A Sabbatical Primer for Churches

How to Love and Honor the Pastor God Has Given You

Written by David C. Alves

with

Marcy Devers Alves

For update information and helpful tips, subscribe to:

David Alves, Author on **Facebook**

and

SabbaticalPrimers.com

Special Limited Offer:

The Kindle, Nook, and PDF versions have live links. For a limited time, anyone who owns the print copy can get a FREE PDF copy of the book with live links to the various articles and resources throughout the eBook and PDF versions.

Simply email me at info@sabbaticalprimers.com with a copy of your receipt for the print version. I will add you to my updates list and reply to your email with the PDF version FREE of charge. I do not sell email lists to any third parties without your permission. You have my word.

A Sabbatical Primer for Churches

Editing by: Jordan Whitlach of Jordy Liz Edits

         Marcy Devers Alves

Cover Photo/Design by: David C. Alves using CreateSpace Cover Designer

David C. Alves's books may be ordered through booksellers or online at:
    CreateSpace.com
    Amazon.com
    BarnesandNoble.com
    Ingram's

Stories in Chapter Six on "The Spouse's Perspective" used by permission.

ISBN-13: 978-1497438743 (CreateSpace-Assigned)

ISBN-10: 1497438748

FIRST PRINT EDITION

PAUPAKPRESS, Concord New Hampshire

Printed in the United States of America

Table of Contents

INTRODUCTION

HEALTHY CHURCHES ARE LED by healthy pastors. How is your pastor's health? How is his or her family's health? Are you encouraging your pastor and pastoral staff to greater health or toward burnout and ministry failure? Are you loving and honoring your pastor by esteeming and providing for his or her spiritual and physical needs or are you stealing ministry by taking what's offered without giving in return? How do you demonstrate your care for the pastor and his or her immediate family?

Have you noticed the toll modern ministry is taking on our pastors? Pastoral fatigue and burnout cost the church more than just money; it costs lives, drying up the pastoral pool. More pastors and church leaders leave ministry today than in the entire history of the Christian Church.

I know because I almost became a statistic.

Now, more than ever, pastors are overwhelmed with demands on their time and energy. They are underwhelmed by congregants willing to do their share and lighten the load.

Though much has been written on the subject of rest, solitude, silence, restoration, and pastoral and clergy renewal, precious few books are available to pastors and churches that *specifically* help them to initiate and successfully navigate a ministry sabbatical. This is especially the case in the church culture that demands so much of its pastors, maintains a tricky balance between rigidity and freedom, and often eyes with suspicion anything that looks even slightly mystical or monastic.

We need to go into the quiet solitude and listen to what the Lord communicates in the great silences of our lives. A spiritual renewal leave or ministry sabbatical provides that sacred space and time with Jesus. Only at maximum risk can a church afford to ignore the spiritual health of its leaders. Those churches that have failed to love and honor their leaders have paid dearly in so many ways, mainly because they are opposing God. And He stands ready to defend His chosen shepherds of the flock.

Our heart and hope is that this primer will revitalize the life of at least *one* pastor and *one* church. If it does, then we have left a legacy of blessing to our fellow pastors, their churches, their families, and our Father. To Christ be all the glory through His body—the Church.

It doesn't get any better than that for authors.

Why This Primer for the Churches?

Pastors are in big trouble, but have few resources to help. Churches served by pastors in trouble are also in trouble. Yet the solution is simple, cost-effective, and honoring to God and the pastoral family.

More and more has been written about sabbaticals, yet few comprehensive, but simple, guidebooks are available to assist a church to initiate and maximize the gift of a pastoral sabbatical for its pastor or pastoral staff. This primer for churches and church leaders is designed to take a church through the sabbatical from conception to conclusion. This book contains more than what was available to our church when I took both my first and second sabbaticals. Though not exhaustive, the contents should accomplish the purpose of a primer on spiritual sabbaticals.

Early in this chapter might be a great place for you to stop and read Pastor Mark Bickford's letter which is linked here and also included in the "Resources for Churches" in the back of the book. It was written to the churches regarding pastoral health and our conference's sabbatical need. It is informational and models the kind of care our pastors and churches receive under the current conference leadership.

What I write, I present not as an expert, but as a pastoral leader and faithful witness who journeys with you and your pastor. Occasionally, as a result of a couple of decades of pastoring, I may wax didactic and get into teacher mode, but forgive me and only take whatever is helpful to you. I wrote this with the prime motives of strengthening your church and blessing your pastor by partnering with you to love and honor your pastor and his or her family.

Above all, I hope to answer some of the questions voiced by some of the churches I've served prior to my previous sabbaticals. Perhaps you already know all about the importance and necessity of a pastoral sabbatical. Great! Please pass this primer on to someone who lacks your awareness and experience—perhaps another leader in your church. Maybe a pastor or close associate is considering a sabbatical (or should consider one) and could benefit from reading this book or my *Sabbatical Primer for Pastors*. You may be planting just the seed your pastor or another church needs.

Who I Wrote For

I wrote this book for any church desiring to experience the renewal and blessing that comes from loving and honoring their leaders in answer to God's mandate. Just as churches are different and have different needs, so pastors are different and have different mindsets. When I wrote *A Sabbatical Primer for Pastors*, I wrote with three types of pastors in mind. This may help you to identify and better help *your* pastor.

The first is the pastor who is convinced he or she needs a sabbatical, but is unsure of where to begin or how to make it the very best experience possible in order to honor the gift of time given by the church or organization granting the sabbatical. If your pastor and church leadership are interested but unsure, and looking for some helpful roadside assistance, this primer is especially for you. I'd like to point you to things that will guide you into and through your pastor's sabbatical. You need to make the most of your pastor's overdue or upcoming spiritual renewal leave. Hopefully, the contents of this primer will help if your pastor fits this first category.

You can also begin by giving him or her a gift of my previous book, *A Sabbatical Primer for Pastors: How to Initiate and Navigate a Spiritual Renewal Leave.* If he or she has a Kindle, it's really easy to go to Amazon.com and gift the book. However, many pastors prefer the print version so that they can write in it or highlight helpful sections.

As your pastor reads the primer for pastors, and you and your leadership read this primer for churches, you can make good progress toward the goal of a successful spiritual renewal leave for your pastor.

The second kind of pastor I have written for is the one who is somewhat interested, whose curiosity is piqued, but feels that he or she has no time for a sabbatical. This pastor's work is so all-consuming that he or she can't possibly break away. This pastor believes the church would fall apart without hands-on pastoring. "No rest for the weary," is this pastor's motto. He or she will not indulge in taking time away from their relentless activity.

Perhaps your pastor is convinced that the Lord's work demands his or her obsessive service. This may have been communicated either by his or her parents, schooling, a previous church, personal makeup or disposition, or . . . *your* church. This pastor needs permission to obey the Lord as He leads them toward a spiritual renewal retreat. If he or she is this obsessive, then your church leadership may need to communicate your concern for the pastor's spiritual, emotional, physical, and, if married, marital health. This primer will help you in that process.

The third kind of pastor is the veteran pastor who understands ministry and knows that he or she is only as effective as their time alone with Jesus. This pastor allows others to take responsibility for ministry. They delegate not out of a sense of laziness, but because they know the wisdom of moving out of the way and allowing others to serve in their spiritual gift areas. This pastor models ministry and calls others to serve out of that quiet solitude and fellowship they experience with the Head of the Church—Jesus. This type of pastor needs little convincing to prioritize renewal and refreshment. This pastor is in ministry for the long haul and has learned that solitude and silence are means to something much greater.

In writing about solitude and silence, Ruth Haley Barton said, "They are not an end in themselves; they are merely a means through which we regularly make ourselves available to God for the intimacy of relationship and for the work of transformation that only God can accomplish."

Perhaps our third pastor has taken one or more sabbaticals already, but keeps a lookout for related resources that may help enlarge or further equip themselves or a fellow pastor for his or her next sabbatical experience. They glean what they can from those who have traveled the same ground and perhaps seen things through different eyes.

No matter which kind of pastor leads your church, they are most likely to benefit from what you'll discover as you read this book to the end. You are well on your way if you recognize your pastor's need for a sabbatical.

So, let's continue.

1 ✦ HOW DID WE GET THERE?

I N 2010, AFTER EIGHT YEARS OF MINISTRY since my first sabbatical in 2002, I experienced depression for no discernible reason. I felt discouraged, defeated, and doubtful that my life situation would get much better.[1] I withdrew from people—church family, friends, and even immediate family. Small tasks loomed huge. Everything took so much mental and physical energy that I didn't know how

---

[1] For those of you who would like to read a more detailed personal account, I have made that available in the resources at the back of the book. See "A Ministry of Pastoral Health: My Testimony."

I could continue in the ministry. Yet I felt very close to the Lord (though He was silent). And I sensed I was still growing spiritually.

Follow that with a TIA (mini-stroke) in the fall of 2011 and my wife's breast cancer gradually getting worse rather than better in the ensuing years, I was hurt, angry, and disappointed. I felt that prayer which produced nothing was a waste of time. I thought no one knew what I was going through. I later found out that my exhaustion showed more than I realized.

The church began to decline. If anything negative could happen that year, it did. Close friends and family, whose children we saw grow from babies to college-age, left our church and flocked to a bigger church in a neighboring town. A faithful core held their ground, but they appeared tired, unsure and complacent. To top it all off, I wasn't sure what the Lord was doing. I only knew that I had to keep following Him no matter what, though I was too disappointed to be enthusiastic about the journey.

Fortunately, at the recommendation of my doctor and in response to my health needs, our church elders granted me a six-month sabbatical—a generous spiritual renewal leave. It had taken a mini-stroke, a mass exodus, and a spiritual winter to get my attention...and theirs. So often, the closest to burnout are the last to know.

Our sabbatical did great things for me and my wife, Marcy, and for the church. Following it, we returned to ministry refreshed, re-inspired, and ready to serve as we had during our early days of ministry. I recovered the strength, optimism, and stamina to re-enter pastoral ministry with new priorities in place and a replenished supply of serotonin. We still have challenges and are in a significant transition from being a building-bound church to the freedom of a house church, but we have learned important lessons from our sabbatical.

I want to maximize the lessons and experiences I had on my first two sabbaticals. I want to capture some of the things that will help us plan our *next* sabbatical. I want to be a good steward of the gift of time away that the Lord and the church gave to us. This book and my primer for pastors have been the means to that end—a place to go to initiate and navigate a successful ministry sabbatical.

Not all pastors are blessed with a congregation that loves and honors them and is willing to demonstrate that love through caring ministry to the pastoral family. The very fact that you're reading this book shows that you and your church want to pursue what is best for your church and pastor(s).

Relatively few congregations understand the unique challenges of ministry and its wearing effects. These effects are not new to ministry. They have existed in ministry since the first century.

Jesus drew away from the strains of ministry often to pray and reflect in lonely places or at His favorite seaside spot in Capernaum. The apostle Paul said that he was constantly weighed down with the issues and concerns of the church. Getting to that place in ministry is not wrong, but staying there is not the answer.

Applauding Exhaustion

Our congregations today often have little idea of how ministry is impacting their pastoral families. Thousands of pastors abandon ministry when they have pushed and worked themselves out of the joy of their calling, or out of their own physical, mental, emotional, and spiritual reserves. Usually, the majority of the congregation has stood by and allowed the undisciplined workaholism of its lead pastor or other pastoral staff to take its inevitable toll. They have applauded from the sidelines, causing the pastor to assume that they desired a pastor aflame with activity. Or perhaps the current or previous pastor modeled workaholism because he or she was taught that nothing short of complete exhaustion was acceptable for serving a needy world.

Our culture in particular inherently applauds and rewards the work ethic that has pushed many church leaders to the point of total exhaustion. Congregations often don't realize how much it costs *them* in terms of broken lives, time wasted, and money squandered in the years it can take to select another pastor whom they can consume—another pastor who will also burn out while meeting the church's needs and often unreasonable expectations.

In his helpful blog post, "7 Reasons Pastors Burn Out," Thom Rainer says, "All pastors would be problem-free if they were omniscient, omnipotent, and omnipresent. Of course, no pastor can meet all the expectations of church members. But many try. And they burn out as a result."

Sometimes brownout or burnout is the pastor's fault. Some pastors believe they're immune to exhaustion. Perhaps they're young, full of vim and vigor, and ignorant of their vulnerability. They mistake *their* stamina for the energy supplied by the Spirit. They may feel great for a while—perhaps a few years, maybe even a decade; but it's only a matter of time before their adrenaline-saturated bodies begin to signal danger on the track ahead. Or perhaps the pastor actually has tied his or her perfectionism to a theology of burning the candle at both ends, based upon what the Apostle Paul said about his being poured out like a drink offering in his ministry to the churches. This produces what looks like tireless, Spirit-led activity, but in reality, it is slavery to an inner voice from somewhere, coupled with a misunderstanding of Paul.

Paul's comments on labor don't often include his own

practice of downtime, which we know he had, often initiated by God himself. Paul began with three years in the prayer closet in Arabia (Galatians 1:17-18). He was imprisoned several times. He traveled, but not by jet plane or train. The travel time of either walking or riding in a cart gave the early disciples and apostles plenty of downtime. Their pace was not usually determined by deadlines and demands. They did not have the same distractions of 21st century ministry—no TV, smart phones, Internet, tablets or other technologies that not only take time to learn, but additional time to maintain. I often wonder if I'm really more productive with all the technology at my disposal. Some days I find that I have spent most of the day looking at screens. Since I use a four-monitor system, that's not an exaggeration.

Jesus' Intent and Example

Paul walked in a unique revelation for the Gentiles, but he also learned from the other Apostles the practices that Jesus had passed on to them. With their own ears, they heard Jesus say, "Come to me all you who are weary and heavily burdened and I will give you REST!" (Matthew 11:28, ESV). Both Jesus and Paul knew the Shepherd that made them lie down in green pastures and led them beside quiet waters (Psalm 23). Jesus, too, had invited His disciples to come aside to rest and refreshment (Mark 6:1). Even though their R&R was interrupted by the constant demands and hounding of the crowds that found Jesus wherever He went (similar to the paparazzi who seek out and hound celebrities), Jesus' original *intent* for them was one of downtime, rest, and quiet reflection in a place separate from the people—solitude, silence, and refreshment.

Our culture worships accomplishment. Our culture bows at the altar of performance. Leaders cannot afford to communicate to their congregations that they approve the cultural performance mentality that pushes them or the congregation to incessantly serve. Pastors often ignore their physical, emotional, and personal spiritual need of adequate rest and downtime, when they should be modeling Jesus' practice of drawing aside and waiting upon the Father to communicate His life choices to His people.

I recently read about a mom's daily schedule in *Sabbath Keeping: Finding Freedom in the Rhythms of Rest* by Lynne M. Baab. At the end of recounting the schedule, Baab writes, "What's going on in our culture, in our world, that a mother with young children believes she's supposed to be active and productive every minute? Why is it scary to think about stopping or slowing down all this relentless activity? Why do we need to justify our existence by constant motion? Why would we think we aren't allowed to rest?"

As I thought about this, a question popped into my mind, *Don't I know pastors like that?*

Assuming that the mom was a believer and attended a church, what do you think her pastor modeled for her to help her break free from the oppression of the performance trap? I asked myself, *What have I been modeling for New Life? Wasn't I like that in the past?*

Your pastor works hard. His or her ministry demands more than most people can imagine. Their time is seldom theirs as they make themselves available to the local church and to others in the community they serve 24/7. Yet I suspect you'll agree that the most important thing a pastor *needs* to do is to remain close to God. Someone once said, "The very nature of being an effective pastor involves continual spiritual growth." Jesus told us that this can only happen while we remain "in the Vine" (John 15:5). Pastors *must* be continually connected to Him to be fruitful.

Your pastor must abide in Jesus if he or she is to have a legitimate, effective ministry for God's Kingdom. All of us who are pastors know how difficult that sometimes can be. The demands are seemingly endless. How can we say we are leading in the Spirit if we're not abiding in the presence of the Lord? The simple truth is: we can't! We often empower and encourage a carnal religious busyness, in place of an anointed, effective ministry.

I've known pastors of small churches who carry huge key chains and do all the building maintenance themselves. They mow, clean, repair, construct and maintain. I've often wondered, *Where do they get the time to do what they're called to do—attend to the Lord and equip the people? How do they give themselves to the ministry of the Word and prayer amidst a flurry of religious and extraneous activities?* These pastors may feel they are being helpful and the congregation may notice and even be appreciative, but in all honesty, the people are being robbed of their opportunity to serve the body. Pastors are not the local church custodians. They are the spiritual leaders of the community of believers gathered in the local churches. What is the pastor's investment in that quiet, vocation of soul care? He or she needs to refocus priorities and establish practices and disciplines that keep him or her in that thin place between this world and the throne room (Matthew 16:23; Colossians 3:1-2).

Verdell Davis, a long-time friend of *Sonscape Retreats*, penned something that powerfully impacted me early in my own sabbatical in 2010. She wrote:

God's call is *first* a call to himself. And such an encounter demands time, silence of surroundings and spirit, and great longing for God himself. When the longing to know him captures our heart, we will search diligently for the time to get away with him to a quiet place. And in that quiet place, silence becomes the womb in which the work of God in our own lives will be birthed to speak a word of hope to a lonely and hurting world.

In our day and age, remaining close to God (given all the demands and distractions of modern culture, both secular and church) is a monumental task. We cannot discover God's intention for our own spiritual formation and the formation of those we're responsible for if we don't give serious time to cultivating our first love.

I'm reminded of a story I once heard and found insightful.

Two lumberjacks went to work for a company. Ted and Jack started the same day in nearby stands of forest trees. Ted cut, chopped, and hacked at trees, unwilling to take even a short break. He wanted to give the owners a good day's work and see if he could out-chop his new fellow lumberjack.

Jack chopped and cut, too, but took a break every couple of hours and actually punched out early. He looked refreshed and invigorated as he passed by Ted still busy at work.

When Ted heard how Jack had gone home early and was affirmed by the bosses, he wondered how much wood the other had cut. To his amazement Jack had cut twice the amount of logs as Ted had. Ted's bosses weren't too happy with his performance and told him they hoped he'd do better the next day.

The next day Ted arrived early and talked with Jack over coffee to learn his secret. Jack said, "Oh, that's basic. I take time every couple of hours to sharpen my ax."

Your pastor works hard. But do you allow him time to

sharpen his axe? You have a responsibility to the pastor you say you love and honor in obedience to God. You have to be his advocate. Your pastor's health and ministry depend upon those who surround him and advocate what Jesus wants for his spiritual formation and health—extended time away alone with Him. Will you decide to help your pastor sharpen his ax?

2 ⋄ THE CALL AND MANDATE

THOUGH THERE ARE SEVERAL SCRIPTURE references to the call of God into the Christian faith, such as 2 Peter 1:10 where believers are encouraged to "make your calling and election sure." *Wilmington's Book of Bible Lists* includes a list of more than 50 Scriptural "callings" issued by God to individuals for specific purposes.

The Pastor's Call

So we know that the concept of a "calling" for service is Scriptural, but where does the idea of the calling of a "pastor" come from? Is this a man-made conception, born out of a late historic accommodation to the organized church? Or by the early rag-tag gatherings of Christians who sought to bring some order to their scattered, and sometimes dysfunctional, groups that needed a hierarchal system to hold it together?

Actually, the idea of religious leaders appointed by God can be traced to the Old Testament with God's appointment of Aaron (brother of Moses) as the priest over the delivered tribes of Israel while they were still in their wilderness wanderings.

Later in Jewish prophetic books, the religious leaders, or priests, were referred to as "shepherds" and the congregants as "sheep." "The shepherds are senseless and do not inquire of the LORD; so they do not prosper and all their flock is scattered" (Jeremiah 10:21).

Jesus reinforced this shepherd and sheep concept by referring to Himself as the "Good Shepherd" and His followers as sheep; also, what later became known as the church, Jesus referred to as the sheepfold.

In the New Testament, God appointed men to lead the church by gifting them and fitting them for the 5-fold spiritual offices (ministries) of and to the family of God.

These apostles, prophets, evangelists, pastors and teachers (or pastor-teachers) are God's gift to us. Christ, the Head of the Church, has placed them in our midst. We may have "called" them to come serve our congregation, but they are not paid employees of an ecclesiastical corporation, the church. They are spiritually gifted, called by the Holy Spirit, prepared for ministry, and placed in the body of Christ just as

Jesus Himself decides (1 Corinthians 12:28-31). They serve Him. By serving Christ in their offices, they serve *us*, His Bride, in love.

A pastor serves out of the authority of love. That is only learned in relationship to Christ and the believing community, not at seminary. Since the mature pastor understands this kind of authority, he or she gives sacrificially and generously to his or her church family. It is the church's responsibility to not abuse that love or take it for granted.

That kind of love has its costs. Among them can be exhaustion, especially following years of self-giving ministry. It's easy to get caught up in caring to the point of forgetting that the ministry belongs to the Lord. We need to help pastors remember that there's only one Savior. And it's not the pastor.

When a pastor has time and space to be alone with Jesus for an extended period, the Lord restores perspective. Jesus is the source of an abundant supply of love and care. When the pastor either reconnects or deepens his bond with Christ, he finds that he can serve more effectively, resulting in more fruit. For apart from Christ, the pastor can do nothing of lasting eternal value.

Scripture requires that the pastor (who by virtue of his calling as an elder) must manage his own family well and see that his children obey him with proper respect (1 Timothy 3:4–5). If anyone does not know how to manage his own family, how can he take care of God's church?

Managing a family well is all about love, wisdom, self-sacrifice, and gentle but firm leadership. In managing the family, a pastor learns the meaning of James 1:5: "If any of you lacks wisdom, he should ask God, who gives generously to all without finding fault, and it will be given to him."

Going to God, hearing for his family, speaking into the lives of those he loves, the bread of God—this is pastoral ministry at its core. This is what Scripture is speaking of when it says that the pastor must answer to God for his watch-care (Hebrews 13:17).

Pastors want to be at their best to serve as under-shepherds of the Chief Shepherd. They are called to a high and holy calling. They carry the people on their hearts. As a result, they carry heavy weights. Listen to Paul on the subject:

Besides everything else, I face daily the pressure of my concern for all the churches. Who is weak, and I do not feel weak? Who is led into sin, and I do not inwardly burn? (2 Corinthians 11:28–29)

. . . how I wish I could be with you now and change my tone, because I am perplexed about you! (Galatians 4:20)

For this reason, since the day we heard about you, we have not stopped praying for you and asking God to fill you with the knowledge of his will through all spiritual wisdom and understanding. (Colossians 1:9)

Few, if any, congregants have been charged with the oversight of the entire congregation.

The Church's Mandate

Respect your pastor's appointment and calling by God to care for the flock—to keep watch over their souls.

Obey your leaders and submit to them, for they are keeping watch over your souls, as those who will have to give an account. Let them do this with joy and not with groaning, for that would be of no advantage to you. (Hebrews 13:17)

Since your pastors and leaders are serving at God's command and by His will, the churches have a responsibility to hear what the Holy Spirit is saying they should do in response. The body of Christ needs to better understand both the nature of the pastoral calling and office, and the outcome for our churches should we get this wrong.

Pastors are not the church's employee or paid CEO. They are appointed by Jesus as spiritual parents who are assigned in the body just as the Holy Spirit wills. Pastors aren't assigned to do all the work and make something happen. They are assigned to train and equip *you* to do the work that brings results (Ephesians 4:11-12).

Pastors who have not yet learned this principle will struggle. They themselves may have some confusion about the nature and focus of their ministry. Some see themselves as hired hands. Churches have misunderstood the nature of ministry because most church members work in a secular environment. Well-meaning congregants have simply applied what they experience in the workplace to the church and to pastors who "run" the church. But the church is not the workplace and it is not a corporation to be "run." It is a family—a family to be led, loved, and treasured. It is a family to be protected from the enemy and the world.

Imagine a family, a mom and kids, who lost their dad—their spiritual leader. So they put out word that they're accepting resumes. They examine the background and qualifications of each candidate, then they find one who looks like he knows how to run an organization well. They "hire" their new dad, one that seems to fit their lifestyle. Preposterous? Of course! Yet that's what some modern churches have done in the hiring of their pastor.

Quite often, so little prayer and discernment goes into the "call" of a new pastor. The church should pray, fast, and be more concerned about the character of the candidate than the qualifications on a resume. They should not only interview the pastoral candidate, but the pastor's family as well. It's a package.

The church that makes a mistake here is in trouble down the road. The pastor who receives the call to an immature church that misunderstands the nature of the pastoral office and calling is also going to be in trouble down the road.

In a healthy congregation, a mutual respect and love develops between congregation and pastors. That is the foundation, built upon Christ, which will ensure effective ministry for the years ahead.

Since pastors are more like spiritual parents than corporate officers, we should have a different way of looking at them and following their example. Hebrews 13:7-8 says, "Remember your leaders, who spoke the word of God to you. Consider the outcome of their way of life and imitate their faith. Jesus Christ is the same yesterday and today and forever."

Notice, we are to "remember" and "consider"—recall and pay close attention to— the "outcome of their way of life." What is their life producing? What are they like? Is Jesus' life evident in theirs? Can we see integrity, spiritual insight and wisdom, and righteousness at work in them? What is the pastor's spouse like? How does his or her relationship with their spouse reflect Jesus? Do they love one another? Is the pastor's ministry at home reflected in the lives of his or her family members? This is a key prerequisite for ministry.

Realize that pastors are human like you: they get tired, need sleep, must eat, get sick, and have personal problems, needs, and desires like you do. Their families need them. They pour themselves out over the complex needs of the people in their congregations. Pastors often blame themselves for the people who leave the fold or for the person that falls in her walk with God.

Pastors are subject to discouragement, doubt, depression, and insecurity about their effectiveness, their relationships with members of the body, and their ability to hold the church together or to meet everyone's needs. As a result, they often cannot remain in ministry, as they succumb to spiritual attack and human discouragement.

In his dissertation on attrition rates and causes in pastoral ministry, Jerry Johnson says:

According to studies by the Alban Institute and Fuller Seminary, 50 percent, fully one out of every two pastors, drop out of ministry within the first five years, and many never go back to the church again. How can the church exert spiritual influence in the nation when her pastors are fatigued, ill, addicted, immoral, worried, and quitting? Does burnout dull their preaching, leadership skills, and teaching?"[2]

---

[2]Jerry Johnson, "An Exploration of Rates and Causes of Attrition Among Protestant Evangelical Clergy in the United States", Dissertation Acadia Divinity College, Acadia University, p. 70, 87.

28

Spiritual Warfare

More and more congregations are coming to terms with what the Word of God teaches with regard to spiritual warfare. Jesus taught that we have a real, though invisible, enemy. That enemy hates God, Jesus, you, your church and your pastor. One of the Lord's purposes for coming to this earth was to destroy the works of that enemy, for "...the reason the Son of God appeared was to destroy the devil's work" (1 John 3:8).

For our struggle is not against flesh and blood, but against the rulers, against the authorities, against the powers of this dark world and against the spiritual forces of evil in the heavenly realms. (Ephesians 6:12)

This battle is very real. Though the enemy targets *you*, understand that pastors are prime targets for his arrows. "'You will all fall away,' Jesus told them, 'for it is written: I will strike the shepherd, and the sheep will be scattered'" (Mark 14:27).

Jesus told His followers that what the enemy did to Him, the enemy will also do to us. The enemy can take far more people out of the battle and victory by striking one shepherd than by having to strike every single person. Be careful that at your church you are not one of the enemy's archers.

In a blogpost in *Charisma* Magazine, "Your Pastor Is Under Attack! What Will You Do?", one pastor recounts why he and his wife left ministry after 30 years:

The constant pressure in our church on top of the painful physical attacks my wife was having almost ate me up emotionally. I became a nervous wreck. I got to the place that I knew if that phone rang just one more time, I'd lose it. So my wife and I packed up and walked away after 30 years of ministry. It tore us up. We still love God, but the constant battles...

If he strikes the pastor, the flock will be in disarray, scattered, and easy pickings. If I were Satan, striking the pastor would be high on my strategy list, with the worship leaders and elders being next.

Your Part: What You Can Do

For those of you to whom spiritual warfare seems fanciful on the one hand, or frightening on the other, I encourage you to:

1. Read your Bible carefully, especially the Gospel accounts to see what Jesus thought about satanic and demonic reality. We have not improved upon or surpassed *His* view of reality. I'd say the Son of God knew more about these things than modern Western skeptics and cynics who prejudicially deny the supernatural. Read Ephesians 6:10ff., along with Luke 10:19.

2. Purchase and read books on spiritual warfare such as *Spiritual Warfare,* by Dr. Philip Payne, and *The Adversary,* by Mark Brubeck.

3. Pray daily for your pastor(s) and other leaders. But don't miss my point in this section: the pastoral vocation is not like other jobs. It is a calling that involves natural and *supernatural* pressures. The toll it can take on pastors is staggering. The hours are long and often unpredictable.

The pastor has many responsibilities outside the congregation as well, including his or her family and extended family.

Pastors need the body. Just like each and every person in the church, pastors need the ministry of God's people. Though some pastors may act as though they don't need anyone's help, the mature ones recognize that attitude as an unhealthy mindset. The mature pastor recognizes the great treasure he or she has in the many gifts, passions, and talents of the people of God. Each person is a treasure. Granted some are gems in the rough, but each person is a diamond and a treasure that was purchased at the price of the precious, shed blood of Jesus. You have a ministry to your pastor. Have you found it yet?

Given God's expectation that we honor, esteem, and make joyful the ministry of pastoral leaders, and given the modern challenges to those leaders and their spiritual and physical health, the church and its leaders need to ask some important questions.

Questions for the Church Body to Answer

Answer these questions for yourself as a church leader:

- Do I love my pastor and his or her family? If so, how do I show that love?

- Am I honoring my pastor as God directs in His written word?

- How do I show it tangibly?

- Am I part of the solution or part of the problem?

- Am I an advocate? In what ways have I protected and provided for my pastor and his or her family? What can I do to help my church and pastor move toward greater spiritual sensitivity and effectiveness?

- When I stand before God, what will I say that I did to fight the good fight with my pastor and/or leaders?

Web Resources

Here are some suggestions as to how you can bless your pastor (and you don't have to wait until "Pastor Appreciation Month" in October):

- How to Say "Thank You" to Your Pastor—Part 1

- How to Say "Thank You" to Your Pastor—Part 2

- Buy your pastor a copy of *A Sabbatical Primer for Pastors* at SabbaticalPrimers.com.

- Read helpful blog posts and resources for pastors and pastors' advocates at PastorsAdvocate.com.

3 ◆ THE NEED

I WROTE THIS PRIMER WITH THREE KINDS of churches in mind.

The first is the church that is convinced their pastor needs a sabbatical, but is unsure of where to begin or how to make it the very best experience possible in order to ensure the maximum benefit for their pastor and the church.

If your pastor is like I was before my first sabbatical, interested but unsure, looking for some helpful roadside assistance, then this primer should help you to assist him or her. I'd like to point you to something that will guide you into and through the pastoral sabbatical. You need to make the most of your pastor's overdue or upcoming spiritual leave. Hopefully, the contents of this primer will help.

The second is the church that isn't quite convinced that helping their pastor take a spiritual renewal leave for three to six months will be a blessing to the church rather than a curse. This church usually desires to honor and do best by its pastor, but simply needs more information or some practical biblical truths, examples, or simply structural suggestions.

A third kind of church actually exists. That church's ministry is likely plateaued or frozen. It has numerous problems. They lack love. They usually don't love or value their pastor enough to care. The pastor is considered an employee. The congregation brings in a pastor, and when they've used him or her up, they simply start the search process again. This pattern repeats itself every three to five years generally. Often a controlling family or faction is active in the background, undermining the pastor's ministry from the moment of their first disagreement.

Unless this church repents, severe discipline will be the result. The Lord may even take away their lampstand. "Away from me you evil-doers, I never knew you," will most likely be the result of their rebellion and apostasy. The church I've just described would probably not benefit from this primer at all because they would likely never read the book. Or if they did, they wouldn't get this far. Loving and honoring the pastor God has given them is not high on their list of priorities.

Your pastor is blessed that his or her church is one of the first two. Now you need only to set your hearts on loving and honoring God first, and then loving and honoring your pastor. Your church is on the way to sowing a blessing into the lives of every member of the congregation.

So, let's launch out.

What Is a Sabbatical?

Let's begin with a definition so that we're on the same page when I use the term "sabbatical." A true sabbatical is not a vacation or holiday season, though these may be added to the beginning, middle or end of a sabbatical.

Primarily, three types of sabbaticals are currently recognized in our western, Judeo-Christian culture at large and can sometimes be confused.

The first is an **academic sabbatical** which is typically not a space of time away for spiritual refreshment or renewal. Academic sabbaticals involve projects of research, study or writing. They are breaks from a highly rigid academic schedule, but not from typical academic work. The person on academic sabbatical leave is simply changing the focus of his or her work, usually to complete writing projects or related research. If you are interested in knowing more about this type of sabbatical, you'll find no shortage of books and articles.

The second type of sabbatical is a **corporate sabbatical**. More and more corporations and businesses of all sizes now recognize the tremendous benefit of a corporate sabbatical. The employee benefits. The company benefits. And profits, rather than being hurt, are increased. An excellent article in *Entrepreneur* magazine enumerating the benefits of this type of sabbatical is "The Refueling Principle," by Joe Robinson.[3] On page 70, it reads:

"As Bhatia has discovered, productivity doesn't come from being glued to the helm every waking moment but from how energized and, as a result, focused and organized your brain is. Humans are just like smartphones or iPods: we have to be recharged, or we run out of juice."

The third type of sabbatical—the one that will receive all of our attention—is a **ministry sabbatical**. Much has been written about the first two. But as of this publication, very little is available for a ministry sabbatical or spiritual renewal leave.

A Spiritual Renewal Leave

A ministry sabbatical is a "spiritual renewal leave." Unlike

---

[3] *Entrepreneur*, October 2014, pp. 67-70.

the other two sabbaticals, it is primarily a time of purposeful ceasing, resting and planned refreshment, with a spiritual renewal component or emphasis. The leave accomplishes a purpose and specific intent: to renew and restore vitality and health—spiritual, emotional and physical—in spiritual leaders. Some element of work may be attached to it, but it would be *different* work than typical ministry responsibilities and tasks. Perhaps the work would be an article, book, or plan for personal or corporate renewal, or perhaps exploring devotional reading and beginning a journal.

How does this differ from the writing of a book that a professor might do on an academic sabbatical? The primary focus of the academic sabbatical is not spiritual or renewal. It is a continuation of the regular academic job description of a professor—to write. The academic sabbatical simply gives them space and more time to do their work.

The writing of a book would be atypical for a pastor. Though some pastors are given the freedom by a congregation to pursue writing as an aspect of their ministry, it is relatively rare. For pastors who do not normally aspire to write books, the writing opportunity can be more like pursuing a hobby or journaling from relaxed reflection.

A trip to Israel or some site of church history might find its way onto the itinerary of a ministry sabbatical. It could involve painting a piece of art or writing a musical composition. I am championing a definition of "ministry sabbatical" as spiritual renewal leave from *ministry,* which could encompass or result in any of the pursuits above.

To me, the primary distinguishing characteristic of the pastoral or ministry sabbatical is a stopping—ceasing of the pastor's day-to-day, ministry-related responsibilities.

A Complete Stop

A ministry sabbatical is ceasing from regular ministry routines and demands. As I previously mentioned, though I have seen no specific command to give an extended season of Sabbath to those in ministry, the sabbatical *principle* is present in Scripture.

Some biblical texts to ponder:

- Genesis 2:2-3—The Hebrew word, *Shabbat,* literally means "ceased" and "stopped."

- Exodus 23:10-12—God built us for a rhythm of work and rest. A ministry sabbatical extends that rest.

- Psalm 23:1-3—As we take some time to enter into the scene, we see that God "makes" the Psalmist "lie down"—cease. Why?

- Psalm 46:10—"Be still" implies stopping. It is in the imperative which means that it is *commanded* by God.

- Psalm 62:1—How does He save us from our ceaseless

activity?

- Hosea 2:14—As you read this text, ask yourself: Who's in the lead? To where? What's the result?

- See Mark B's letter. In "Resources for Churches."

The Hebrew word *Shabbat*, used by God in Genesis, is really a stopping or ceasing more than a rest. God never tires. He did not rest on the seventh day. He is the One who never sleeps nor slumbers. He needs no rest. Bible translators would have better served us to stay closer to the denotative definition of the Hebrew than to have made it seem that God just took a short breather or nap. He *ceased* from His work. He *stopped* what He was doing. That is what He meant to communicate. Therefore, that is what He calls us to do on our Sabbath—make an abrupt end of our labor. All labor? No, our *usual* labor—the labor we've been doing the other six days of the seven-day week.

A ministry sabbatical is not a vacation. It is a different kind of work; it is a directed time of refreshment and restoration. It is a time for drawing closer and listening more carefully, with the intent of deeper intimacy with God. It can involve reading, writing, and wrestling in prayer—especially wrestling with the tendency to be busy, wrestling to let go, to jump off the performance-go-round, and relax. For some, it takes great effort to cease working in the normal sense.

A spiritual renewal leave is also an intentional release

from stressors and overwhelming spiritual drains and people-demands. It's also a recharging of the biological battery.

Serotonin is a neurotransmitter essential not only to your survival, but to your sense of well-being and vascular health. Prolonged stress depletes serotonin levels. Once a person's levels are depleted, those levels are not restored by a good night's sleep.

In his important book, *Leading On Empty*, Pastor Wayne Cordeiro recounts the advice of his psychologist friend regarding serotonin levels. My physician agreed with Wayne's friend that the process to regenerate serotonin to healthy levels is more like the trickle-charge on a boat or motorcycle battery. The body needs extended time to produce what the body needs. That's one of the reasons my doctor recommended to the elders that I take six months away for my 2010 sabbatical. Unless you take adequate time away from ministry required to maintain good levels, your battery cannot fully recharge. I'm not suggesting that every sabbatical needs to be six months, but three seems to be the minimum for adequate physical and spiritual renewal.

This is no longer the ministry world of the 18th and 19th century village parson. Someone could convincingly argue that if contemporary pastors observed a regular, weekly Sabbath—ceasing from doing anything on a "to do" list and resting fully—they would not need a three- to six-month sabbatical. I'm currently testing that hypothesis, and have been since my last sabbatical. I'm doing that by observing a weekly Sabbath with my wife. Perhaps in 2015, when five years since my last sabbatical is up, I won't need a sabbatical at all. We'll see.

A newsletter from the Louisville Institute, a Lilly Endowment funded program, says, "Sabbatical is a gift to renew you as a person, marked by deep rest rather than to-do lists, projects, or products."

An Opportunity for Others to Share in Ministry

Rather than feel threatened by others ministering in his place—other staff, members of the congregation, or supply personnel—the secure leader can use the ministry sabbatical leave as an equipping opportunity. Others have to step up to the plate. An insecure leader or pastor fears losing ground, but a mature, confident leader sees his or her sabbatical as the opening for greater responsibility to be carried by potential and veteran leaders alike.

Why a Sabbatical?

Why should your pastor take a sabbatical? If you've been a Christian long enough, or had a personal acquaintance with your pastor or pastoral families, I shouldn't have to answer this for you. If you are already convinced and have considered the scriptural support for a sabbatical, then go directly to the next section. But let's assume for a moment that you honestly don't know whether or not a sabbatical has any legitimate spiritual or biblical support and would like some background. Or let's suppose you're someone who feels that your pastor should operate under the assumption: *I'll never tire or need a sabbatical.* Hopefully what follows will challenge that way of thinking.

Though the word or term *sabbatical* cannot be found in Scripture (as is the case with the word *Trinity*), the principles and models are there. As a matter of fact, we glean our current understanding of sabbatical rest from glimpses we see of it throughout Scripture—the clear teaching of Sabbath texts—and from the life of Jesus.

A Hermeneutical Viewpoint

How you arrive at doctrine (biblically-based behavior) from the Word is a huge part of how you view not only Scripture, but the effects of the atonement. I was told by one of my seminary professors that Calvin and Luther approached doctrinal questions in two very different ways.

Calvin: If the practice or object isn't addressed in Scripture, then it is not permissible.

Luther: If it is not forbidden in Scripture, then it is permissible.

You can see how Calvin's view impacted church doctrine

and subsequent history for him and his followers. In Geneva, Calvin did not allow instruments that were not in the Bible. Singing in harmony was not permitted. A pipe organ would likely have been out of the question. If he were alive today, drums, electric guitars, harmony, and parking lots would be anathema! As would Honda Civics, the E-Z Pass, and kitchen blenders. A strain of legalism continues in many churches today as a result Calvin's premise.

Luther understood that God has given us freedom in Christ (Galatians 5:1-3). This understanding is crucial to the body of Christ so that we do not end up under the Christian law. Luther allowed for vocal harmony and musical instruments not mentioned in Scripture. And I can only guess that he might have enjoyed having an E-Z Pass in his Honda Civic as he drove from home to the church parking lot. Maybe he would have appreciated satellite radio, too.

Since God's intent and prescription was that we prioritize a weekly Sabbath day (one in seven) throughout the entire year, how much more do full- and part-time ministers need to have an *extended* Sabbath rest every fifth or seventh year, depending on what your church agrees upon regarding frequency?

Since Sabbath principles abound in Scripture, as we illustrated earlier in this chapter, and since a sabbatical is not forbidden, then we are free to establish and practice the biblical principle of a time to "come away" and be with Christ to debrief, and be rested, renewed, refreshed, and restored in body, spirit, and soul. This is especially crucial since many pastors I know have not ceased their ministries for even one day in seven. I repeat: *Because a sabbatical is not forbidden in Scripture, we are free to include it in our practice of ministry.* I would argue that the same is true of a weekly Sabbath day for God's people—including the pastor. And no, Sunday is not a Sabbath for the pastor and his or her family. As a result of how tiring Sunday ministry is, another day of the week should be chosen as a day of Sabbath rest. Scripture can be our best source for determining our view with regard to Sabbath and sabbaticals.

As a matter of fact, we glean our current understanding of sabbatical rest from glimpses we see of it throughout Scripture in the Sabbath and wilderness texts. We also see it from the history of Judaism forward into the life and teachings of Jesus to His disciples and the church, and throughout church history up until the late twentieth century.

By the way, don't feel resentful or envious when the Lord directs your pastor to go off by himself for extended time. This is one of Christ's patterns for spending time with us. Being much alone with Jesus is why churches set pastors apart and provide that opportunity.

John the Baptist went out to the desert. Jesus was led into

the wilderness to be tempted by the devil. Interestingly, it wasn't the devil that "led" Him out there. Who did? The Holy Spirit (Luke 4:1-2).

What about newly converted Saul of Tarsus (the apostle Paul? Where did he go after his Damascus road experience and subsequent healing? He spent three years in the spiritual (and perhaps literal) desert since he was in Arabia—alone, in solitude, to hear from the Lord (Galatians 1:11-20). There he learned the Gospel which he heard by revelation (not from people) but from the Lord along with all that he would suffer for Christ in his future ministry (Acts 9:15-16). God gives guidance and revelation when we get aside with Him (James 1:5-8)

The wilderness is the place where God gets our full attention. This is where He prepares our arm for battle. "But God led the people around by the way of the wilderness toward the Red Sea. And the people of Israel went up out of the land of Egypt *equipped for battle*" (Exodus 13:18, ESV, emphasis mine).

The wilderness is also the place He brings His people so that they are immersed in the quiet where He can speak, and they can hear and respond to His loving initiative. "But then I will win her [Israel] back once again. I will lead her into the desert and speak tenderly to her there" (Hosea 2:14, NLT). It's really hard to hear in our noisy, demanding culture. We need the solitude of the wilderness to better hear what the Spirit is saying to the churches.

How much time has your church body spent in the desert? Any wonder you and I seldom operate from the kind of revelation or illumination that those mentioned in the Scriptures experienced? Make plans to give your pastor room to dream and discern; allow him or her to be purposeful in spending time alone and quiet with your heavenly Father on a sabbatical.

A Sabbatical Was Commanded by God

At creation, Yahweh designed people such that they would need to cease their activities one day in seven. He said, too, that even the land needed rest and refreshment. He is our Creator. He, better than anyone, knows we need rest and a ceasing from our labor:

God's Prescription for His Land

In Scripture, the key Hebrew concept is *Shemitah*—the seventh (Sabbath) year. Farmland was to be farmed six years then left fallow on the seventh. The rest for the land restored its nutritive power and assured better crops. Whatever grew up from it uncultivated also fed the poor. Both land and people benefited.

For six years you shall sow your land and gather in its yield, but the seventh year you shall let it rest and lie fallow, that the poor of your people may eat; and when they leave the beast of the field may eat. You shall do likewise with your vineyard and with your olive orchard. Six days you shall do your work, but on the seventh day you shall rest; that your ox and your donkey may have rest; and the son of your servant woman and the alien may be refreshed. (Exodus 23:10-12)

If God so cared for the land by commanding a full year of lying fallow (no planting) after every sixth year, does He care for His children any less than the land?

God's Prescription for His People

God calls us to rest and quiet in order to be renewed.

For thus said the Lord God, the Holy One of Israel, "In returning and rest you shall be saved; in quietness and in trust shall be your strength." But you were unwilling... (Isaiah 30:15, ESV, emphasis mine)

The LORD is my shepherd; I shall not want. He makes me lie down in green pastures. He leads me beside still waters. He restores my soul. He leads me in paths of righteousness for his name's sake. (Psalm 23:1–3, ESV, emphasis mine)

God established a Sabbath Day. We are to work six days, and then we and our households (including the animals) are to have total rest the seventh day—to stop and cease. "He makes me lie down," says the Psalmist. "He leads me beside still waters." None of these scenes suggest busyness as something to be more highly valued than solitude, silence, or rest. I've spoken to many pastors through my various responsibilities. Most pastors have seldom or never taken a Sabbath Day of rest. This is also clear from the large number of them leaving ministry altogether. The most recent statistic I saw was 1,200 pastors leaving ministry each month. Some may be leaving through retirement, but that's not the impression I got from the research.

Pastors are increasingly exhausted by the challenges and difficulties of modern ministry, yet few have cared for their own spiritual needs by taking a dedicated, weekly Sabbath day. To have observed a Sabbath would have given them 52 Sabbath days of ceasing, rest and refreshment prescribed to them by God. Some of the guys I've known have confessed that they usually run errands and do chores that day. That is not a ceasing from their labor, so it's little wonder that they can't wait to get back to work; and, when they do, they're still in need of a Sabbath rest.

Jesus never nullified the Sabbath. We do not need to legalistically observe it for our salvation, but Jesus warned that we were not to do away with it. Anyone who does or teaches that the Sabbath is no longer holy to the Lord for the purpose of our refreshment, is least in the Kingdom. "Therefore whoever relaxes one of the least of these commandments and teaches others to do the same will be called least in the kingdom of heaven, but whoever does them and teaches them will be called great in the kingdom of heaven" (Matthew 5:19, ESV).

We are to keep its original intent in mind when we practice it. "And he said to them, 'The Sabbath was made for man, not man for the Sabbath'" (Mark 2:27, ESV).

Jesus goes on to say in Mark 2:28 that He is "Lord even of the Sabbath." Would He be Lord of something that no longer exists or has significance? Sabbath rest continues to be a much misunderstood and neglected biblical practice.

God's Prescription for His Leaders

Church leaders carry responsibilities and weights that exceed those of most other professions or societal roles. That may be why God, under the Old Covenant, required the priests to retire at age 50 and become coaches of the younger men.

And the Lord spoke to Moses, saying, "This applies to the Levites: from twenty-five years old and upward they shall come to do duty in the service of the tent of meeting. And from the age of fifty years they shall withdraw from the duty of the service and serve no more. They minister to their brothers in the tent of meeting by keeping guard, but they shall do no service. Thus shall you do to the Levites in assigning their duties." *(Numbers 8:23–26, ESV)*

Unlike the Levites who served the Tabernacle, pastor's weights are not physical, though they can affect us physically.

Our burden and service is spiritual, emotional and mental. These weights take a greater toll than physical weights. They include:

- 24-hours-a-day concern over individuals and families in crisis

- Endless meetings and people sessions

- Church conflict resolution

- Home and family responsibilities

- Spiritual warfare—both overt and covert, not to mention extremely oppressive

- Denominational or associational responsibilities

- Continuing educational responsibilities or requirements

- Chronic relational challenges in some leadership teams

- On call night and day; 24/7/365 (even while on vacation)

- Ministry of the Word study and preparation—worship services, Bible studies, visitation, counseling times, community obligations, broadcasts

- Physical challenges—personal chronic illness, physical limitations, caregiving for family members and/or aging parents

Jesus called His disciples to "come away" with Him to a quiet place for the purpose of rest (Mark 6:31). Your pastor, too, needs to get away with the Lord for an extended time of decompression from the adrenaline overdose.

Though Jesus, no doubt, observed a weekly Sabbath, He withdrew for 40 days (and other extended periods) for the purpose of equipping, fellowship with His Father, intercession, and listening. He regularly followed teaching times in the temple with time in the country or lakeside.

A Sabbatical Is an Investment in Your Pastor's Continued and Future Ministry

Too many pastors leave their assignments too soon. Some churches don't care. Shame on them. They have disobeyed God. Other churches are careful to keep and help their pastors to optimum spiritual health. That is where God's blessing descends and remains. They care for their pastors by investing (sowing) a sabbatical, or a spiritual renewal leave, into the equation. It becomes God's gift of grace to the receiving pastor, and ultimately, to the church. In Lynn Baab's book, *Sabbath Keeping: Finding Freedom in the Rhythms of Rest,* she says, "The purpose of the Sabbath is to clear away the distractions of our lives so we can rest in God and experience God's grace in a new way."

Have you ever felt like you needed a touch from the Lord? That if only you could experience Him afresh you would have all that you need to face what life hands you? Your pastor also needs and desires such new encounters. You contribute fruitfulness to your pastor's service to the body by granting him or her the freedom to invest dedicated time to enlarge vision, to deepen passion, and to refresh mind and spirit. By sowing a sabbatical into the life of your pastor, you sow quality and quantity time aside with the Lord; you help to renew his or her passion and vision. This in turn renews the church.

A sabbatical is an extension of weekly Sabbath rest. Granting a ministry sabbatical to build up or renew your pastor's spirit may prevent him or her from leaving the ministry before it is God's time to do so.

The dark time I experienced made me think my ministry had come to an end, but the Lord showed me that it was His way of drawing me away from my props to fully lean into Him. What if I had left the ministry before I carved out that time? Now my church, my wife, and I are experiencing the blessing of the Lord because He refreshed us enough to endure and persevere. He strengthened us. He more closely attuned us to His voice through the silence and solitude our sabbatical made possible. He has given me clarity and vision for the church to make the most of the challenging times ahead.

Your pastor may have hit a rough spot, but that isn't necessarily an indication he or she should leave the post. Perhaps the Lord simply wants their full attention during an extended renewal leave, so he or she can gain courage for the coming years. Yet without time away from ministry, your pastor may believe that the only way out of the present challenges is to resign from the post.

A Sabbatical Is Your Act of Love for Your Pastor and Your Pastor's Family

Pastors must give time not only to personal study, message preparation, and equipping, but to human need—spiritually and temporally—week after week, year after year. This level of output requires that the pastor's greatest work is to believe further into Jesus (John 6:28-29). This takes an investment of time. To know the Father and Son more intimately is our most important work. Intimacy takes time and determined effort. Spiritual attentiveness and growth in love is the well from which pastors draw water to first refresh their own family, then the flock; love and ministry begin in the pastor's home. Often a pastor's time and energy is so depleted in serving the church that there is little left for spouse and family.

For those of us who pastor, our foremost credential is not our seminary education or our knowledge of the Bible or some other knowledge or our personal abilities or spiritual experiences; our most important credential is our family. How a man or woman relates to his or her family demonstrates whether or not he or she should be in ministry. If I don't love and honor my father and mother, then I dishonor God. If I can't live in understanding with my spouse, then how will I be confident of answered prayer in my life (1 Peter 3:7)? If I exasperate my children instead of bringing them up in the training and admonition of the Lord, how can I ever manage a family of families—the church of God (1 Timothy 3:4-5)? Show me a dysfunctional family in the parsonage and I'll show you an unhealthy church. Those loving traits that ensure the home is in order are the same traits necessary to successful, effective church ministry.

But how do we so love our families that they become a model of the body of Christ?

We treasure them!

We must love and treasure each one. Communicating and fostering such love takes time and presence. Not just "quality time," but *quantity* time. We must be *with* them. Live with them and their needs, their desires, their flaws and failures. Listening to their heart-needs. Listening to the Father for them. Seeking His wisdom for each person in the family.

Ministry as it is currently practiced in our nation does not usually value or applaud time alone with God or time invested in the family. This is a huge problem that needs to be addressed. Loving your pastor and his/her family involves protecting their need for family time through encouraging a Sabbath day once a week and providing a renewal leave—a ministry sabbatical—every five to seven years.

If parents could prevent their child from wandering from the faith by merely prioritizing one day a week as a family day of rest and refreshment, focusing on the Lord as they live life together, don't you think that choice would be an investment worth making?

Encouraging and providing for a sabbatical would allow for a larger block of family-centered as well as God-centered time from which the pastor and family will reap many benefits.

Here are a few:

1. Individual break time to draw closer to the Lord and each other.
2. Time to refocus on the family dynamics and make course adjustments.
3. Opportunity for family bonding.
4. Atmosphere for open, honest conversation and assessment of where each *individual* family member is: content or discontent, happy or sad, thriving or in need of help.
5. Assessment of where the family unit is as a whole: Are we in this ministry together? Is anyone feeling disconnected or overlooked?
6. Family fun-time with no guilt . . . time to laugh together free of ministry expectations, weights, and burdens. Often the pastoral family feels guilty when

they take time for themselves for fun. That need not be if the congregation makes it clear that it supports recreational time for the pastoral family.

7. Time to seek God together and pray for one another's needs as a family.

8. Opportunity to reconnect with the extended family without feeling the pull of "getting back to work" or dealing with church family worries while away.

9. A time to heal physically, mentally, and emotionally. A loving congregation will be aware that not only the pastor but his or her family members need an extended break from life in the fish bowl.

For a first-hand view of how a sabbatical can and does minister to the pastor's family, read the next chapter

4 ♦ THE SPOUSE'S PERSPECTIVE

Compiled and Edited by Marcy Alves

WHEN DAVID WAS WORKING FEVERISHLY to complete his book, *A Sabbatical Primer for Pastors,* we both agreed that there needed to be a version of the book geared toward church congregations and decision makers. We realized that it is one thing for a pastor to realize his need of a rejuvenating break from ministry, but it's another matter to bring the congregation to see that need. And not only to see the need, but to make a way for their pastor (and other full-time church leaders) to take a spiritual renewal leave from ministry—free from the stresses of day-to-day ministry, and the concern of no longer having a job when they returned. It was then that *A Sabbatical Primer for Churches* was birthed.

After the first of the companion books was completed, I asked David if he would be interested in having me write a chapter in the new book. He suggested that we co-author the book.

David has been a pastor for over 25 years, and I have, during that time, been a pastor's wife. I wanted the opportunity to share my perspective on the wear-and-tear of pastoral ministry—spiritually, emotionally and physically. Since my husband recognizes the stresses of pastoral life are shared by spouse and family, he agreed it would be a good idea to include a chapter from the pastor's wife's perspective, along with personal testimonies from other pastor's wives, regarding the effects of the constant stress of ministry on their husbands, their children and themselves. Along with me, these wives have experienced the benefit of a caring congregation, who not only saw the need for a pastoral sabbatical, but enabled that to happen through financial support. I'll begin with my story.

From Itinerancy to Local Church Ministry

I have been "in ministry" since I first became a Christian in junior high, as I tried to convince my peers and my family members of their need of the Savior. I attended a four-year Bible college in Philadelphia preparing for a life of ministry.

I believed, and still do, that everyone needs to meet Jesus by personal faith. Leading others to Him has been an important part of my call to ministry.

I was involved in music ministry for several years after college before I met David. After we were married, we began to minister together—first in music and youth work, then in an itinerant ministry of renewal for local churches. We also hosted "Come Away" events for couples in pastoral ministry. But we did not have personal experience with the toll that pastoral ministry takes on the couple and their family, except through second-hand reports.

In the large youth organization of which I was a member in high school, I had been voted "most likely to be a pastor's wife." After several years of itinerant ministry, I thought I would enjoy being a pastor's wife, to enjoy the stability of a local congregation, get off the road from itinerant ministry, end the miles of driving from event to event, equipment set-up, etc. But, I had no idea of the cost of pastoring. Though the traveling ministry had its workload, it also had its perks: gracious receptions, gratitude for our ministry, applause, appreciation, encouragement, being well thought of. The people who didn't like us or our ministry didn't usually vocalize it to us, so the feedback was mostly positive. We were young and we had energy. And there seemed to always be fruit from each ministry. We established great friendships over the years with people we led to Jesus or encouraged in their faith walks.

The time came when we both tired of travel and put feelers out for the possibility of a position in pastoral ministry. We began with a cell church pastorate that started with a handful of folks who were tired of the traditional church scene (they had been burned in a rather liberal church in Massachusetts). That church plant began with a few couples and their children as a Bible study at one of their homes. We all decided to follow the cell church model. The church grew large enough that we began to rent a facility for Saturday night contemporary services. Then the attacks came from the enemy, and due to our lack of pastoral experience, the church had a split and our pastorate there ended. We had several offers to pastor in other places—one was a large, established, more traditional church setting on the West Coast; another was a church similar to the one we left, which was located on the East Coast. The second church desired to become a cell-based fellowship; we thought it was the best fit for us and it kept us in closer proximity to our families.

This second pastorate had an awesome start and there seemed to be excitement over our acceptance of the position. But we soon found that this fellowship was not without significant underlying problems. Though the leadership was made up of unified, godly men, there were several different ideas about the direction the church should take. Additionally, conflicts existed in the congregation over doctrine. Other issues were also uncovered, such as infidelity among members of the worship team, a cross-dresser on the worship team, marital problems, family issues, and, at a later date, a case of child-molestation. There were a couple members who had desired the pastoral position which my husband had been called to fill, who were sometimes divisive; there were others who had divergent ideas on what style of worship we should have. The list goes on.

The church met in a school cafeteria on Sunday mornings, which required set-up and tear-down every week as the responsibility of the worship team and a few volunteers. At a later date, the body voted to purchase a small building as a temporary space where we would not have to do the weekly set-up and tear-down for worship, the children's ministry, and the nursery. The building also afforded us a place for other church activities. It was also at congregational capacity when we first moved in.

Though the elder team remained strong, we began to feel the effects of a space too small for our needs. There was also a lot of burnout among our cell group leaders, who usually doubled in other areas of service. As in most churches, about 15 percent of the people did the work and the rest were along for the ride. I don't say that with any animosity; it's just how it is in most churches today, regardless of the size of the congregation. Often it's, "Meet my needs," instead of, "How can I help meet the needs of others?"

Whether it was from unmet expectations of the congregation, our own perception of their expectations, the weekly "non-traditional church" worship sameness, the loss of our key worship leaders to a larger church in town, or the slow trickle-out of key members who wanted more programs for their children than New Life was able to provide from our small pool of gifted workers, these disappointments added to normal ministry stress and took a toll on both David and me.

As people left for larger churches and our pool of workers shrunk, I began to pick up more of the workload: worship team member, children's church teacher, nursery worker, seminar teacher, and congregational communications. Wherever there was a need, I filled in, even filling in with the sermon presentation on occasion. I loved serving in worship, I loved the kids, and I enjoyed speaking and preaching, but ministry stress eventually took its toll.

I could also see my husband getting discouraged, second-guessing whether he should continue in pastoral ministry at New Life or even *at all*. He periodically talked of quitting the pastorate. Ordinarily, David is a very positive person—a joyful optimist, a people lover, very outgoing—but he began to avoid people and spending more time in the evening in his "man cave" room at home playing computer games.

I was diagnosed with breast cancer and within two years David had a TIA—a mini-stroke. His primary care doctor recommended an extended break from ministry for three to six months, and wrote a letter stating the same to our elders.

About seven years earlier, the congregation had given us a two-month sabbatical, which included some of our regular vacation time, and they had seen the benefit of that break for us and for them. Fortunately, we still had a good core group of supportive members and elders who led the way for David to be able to take what was now obviously a much-needed sabbatical. One of our elders, who had been team-pastoring with David part-time, took over church leadership and did some of the preaching while David was out of the pulpit. He did a good job pastoring the people. We also had outside pulpit supply lined up for some of the Sundays.

I have often wondered that if we had added children to our mix of that ongoing stress, how much that time would have adversely affected them. We had earlier in that pastorate hosted several foreign students, but our own adopted daughter was away at college and on her own for the most part. Additionally, we offered temporary housing to some adults who were homeless. But our "kids" were not small children who wondered where their dad was when they needed him, such as the case in many pastoral homes. This pastor-dad absence has often led to pastors' kids breaking rank, going into depression, or opting for rebellion—to the heartbreak of their parents—and has resulted in dire effects on the pastor's ministry to the church body.

Pastoral ministry not only produces physical and mental stress for pastors and spouses, but emotional drains and spiritual attacks are constant. We are dealing not only with daily prayer, study, and message preparation, but of ministries to individuals with varying degrees of spiritual maturity (or immaturity), and to their mental, emotional, physical, temporal and spiritual needs. Additionally, we have a very real enemy who, Jesus told us, is out to "kill, steal, and destroy" (John 10:10).

Full-time Christian workers seem to be in rescue mode constantly, often experiencing their own spiritual attacks as they seek to encourage, mentor, and aid others in finding spiritual freedom. We experience intense spiritual warfare when we are even attacked in our dreams by dark spirits. There are times when darkness attempts to suck us into depression, discouragement, or doubt regarding the effectiveness of our ministries to others, or our ability to hear from God.

Pastors, their wives, and their families often experience abandonment by those very people in whom they have invested their lives. Recently, another minister's wife asked me how I handle it when people who have been a part of our church "family" that we seek to serve, suddenly jump ship and drift away to another church fellowship in the same town or one nearby. Some declared that New Life is "just the church they have been looking for." Three to six months later, they have disappeared. Others have announced to the congregation, "God has shown me that this is my church family." Their subsequent disappearance always makes us wonder how God changed His mind so quickly.

What do we do about the sadness that feels like personal rejection, a divorce, or sometimes even a death? How about when you feel that people are not being honest about why they are leaving? For most pastors' wives, many tears are shed.

I shared with that pastor's wife, mentioned in the last paragraph, that David and I have agreed to remain open and friendly to those who have left the "family." We haven't stopped caring about them, nor do we break off fellowship, as long as they desire to maintain it. We do not go after people who choose to leave; we continue to minister to those who remain. The church is Christ's, not ours.

How does the pastor feel when he or she preaches his or her heart out week after week, but people don't seem to get it? Or if they do, they don't apply what they are being taught? This, too, is another stress of pastoral ministry that most dedicated pastors experience, and we were no exception to the rule.

To continue my personal story, it had been about seven years since our previous two-month vacation and sabbatical when we both experienced the health problems mentioned earlier in this chapter. We both needed a break. Though I was concerned with good reasons about the welfare of the church body while we were on sabbatical, we really needed a time of personal rest and refreshment, a time to focus on the Lord and on each other, and a time to regain our health on every level. Most of the members continued to support our associate pastor while we were away; some left during our absence, finding that easier than talking to us about why they felt the need to move on.

We had no personal financial resources to cover our extended sabbatical. Our church elders voted to continue to pay David's salary while we were on sabbatical, and our local association of churches, Maranatha Conference, helped financially by paying our way to a ministry retreat place. We also had friends who personally helped with travel, housing, and other expenses.

We spent the first couple of weeks at home planning an itinerary. We knew we needed to be away from our home setting and our church services. We visited other churches on Sundays so we could experience ministry from other pastors. We tried to remain uninformed of any church difficulties at our church fellowship during this time at home and during our remaining sabbatical time away. We visited friends and relatives in other states, stayed for several weeks at my parents' summer lake house in Pennsylvania, visited the Jersey Shore, and experienced the ministry of *Sonscape*

Retreat Center in Divide, Colorado—a beautiful retreat setting focused on ministering to couples in pastoral fatigue or burnout. We each came away from *Sonscape* with a word of caution from the counselors: for David, "There is only one Savior and you're not Him," and for me, "Don't let anybody 'should' on you, including yourself."

When we returned from our six-month sabbatical, my husband was a different man from when we left for sabbatical. He had his old energy and enthusiasm back. So did I. We were expecting great things to happen in our fellowship.

It was very telling upon our return to the church that the pastor-elder who had filled in for David needed a sabbatical—which was granted to him. Because he was bi-vocational, he supported himself financially for that sabbatical; but it took him longer to recuperate from the stress of ministry, since he still had to go to work each day. He left our fellowship shortly after his sabbatical ended, to attend another church where, for several years, he was free from all leadership responsibility.

During our time at *Sonscape*, we decided that, from then on, we would take one day a week for our personal Sabbath day—not a normal day off to run our errands and catch up on personal stuff, but a time of *ceasing* to gaze inward at our heart-needs and at the Lord. We have mostly held to that since our return from the last sabbatical; we spend both personal and couple-time in prayer and listening to the Lord; it's our time for spiritual refreshment. We enjoy it as a day of relaxation.

The members of our fellowship respect that day for us and don't contact us with problems, unless there is an emergency. We wish we had known how much it would have saved us physically, spiritually, and emotionally to have carved out that weekly Sabbath early in pastoral ministry.

My reflections on our previous ministry exhaustion, consequent need for a sabbatical, and its outcome are my personal experience; other pastoral spouses will have different stories of sabbaticals and the results of their hiatus from pastoral ministry. I have asked four other pastors' wives who have recently taken ministry sabbaticals with their husbands to share their experiences.

Sabotaged by Realities: Catherine, Merrimac, NH

Is it okay to admit that ministry has begun to feel like just a chore rather than a joyful calling? That an unhealthy stress level has led me to feeling physically exhausted most of the time? That there is no emotional cushion to absorb yet another setback or disappointment? That daily activity is directed by autopilot rather than purposeful motivation? That having no margin in the schedule has resulted in feeling trapped in reactive responses, rather than proactive planning, and therefore reducing one's focus from passionate pursuit of priorities to merely maintaining the mundane? That minimal self-care and spouse care has produced relational, physical, and emotional ill health, with no time or desire to think and discuss what and how things need to change?

This is the state in which Roger and I found ourselves in the spring of 2013. We were aware of our needy condition, but did not realize that it had become so apparent to family and ministry associates. We are grateful for the love of various individuals who recognized our need and took steps to intervene and provide help to regain our health and balance.

God's love demonstrated through His people resulted in many generous blessings! These converged into a four-month sabbatical, during which time we were released from church ministry responsibilities in order to devote ourselves and our energies to diagnose the causes which contributed to our circumstances and to determine needed corrections to our lifestyle. This extended time to "unstring the bow" yielded many positive results.

Rest: Nearly the entire first month was spent recovering from exhaustion. Allowing ourselves to step off the treadmill revealed how very tired we were; we could hardly keep awake for more than a few hours. This month provided me with necessary time to recover from a severe respiratory illness and dental surgery, both requiring prescriptions and antibiotics, plus a bout with the intestinal flu. Roger, my husband, needed to recover from prolonged depletion of energy as he was running on empty. Our awake hours provided time for reading and journaling, which helped clarify our individual purposes, passions, and priorities.

Rejuvenation: Our second month included the wonderful opportunity to experience *Sonscape,* a week-long retreat for ministry couples in the incredibly picturesque setting of Divide, Colorado, with the ever-present view of Pike's Peak! This retreat enabled us to interact with other ministry couples and with seasoned counselors who understood the demands of ministry life and our dynamic as a couple. It provided voices and resources outside the scope of our personal settings, offering loving empathy, perspective, and challenging counsel for individual needs. It also provided soothing hospitality, comfortable accommodations, and home-cooked family-style meals. We remember saying at our exit interview, that "it felt as if a log-jam had been released," allowing communication to flow more freely—even honest conversations which included some uncomfortable ones as we addressed sensitive issues.

Recreation and Restoration: Our third month provided opportunity for us to enjoy time at our rustic cottage, a place rich in family history, where we both sigh with contentment upon arrival and receive benefits of its simple, therapeutic environment. During this time, we reconnected with friends and family whom we seldom see, and continued with reading and journaling. This month also provided the desperately needed opportunity to repaint the cottage and to enjoy the sense of completion of a project, in contrast to the ongoing nature of ministry work.

Renew and Reset: Our fourth month was spent at home. Long-delayed home projects were attended to which had been previously difficult to find time or motivation to accomplish. We endeavored to implement reformed goals for our personal and joint schedules and activities, as well as a makeover of our physical environment.

Return: When the time came for us to return to "active duty," we were welcomed back with enthusiasm by the majority of the church family (though a few maintained the position that they saw no necessity of a pastoral sabbatical). Roger feels that he might not have continued in ministry in our present location if it were not for this sabbatical relief. Many expressed that they observed improvement in Roger's overall health, color, and energy, which resulted in more efficient time-management, a benefit both personal and for the church. Things Roger had processed through reading, journaling, and prayer became sharply focused and resulted in passionate preaching as he shared the perspectives and vision God had given him.

Another positive sabbatical impact was the preparation and adoption of new church by-laws implementing elder leadership of the church body. This decision has resulted in changes in attendance and support as the church moves forward in this elder-led emphasis.

During our absence, the church also witnessed the power of "homegrown" leadership, using the New Testament model. During our four-month Sabbatical, our son, Joshua, preached all but two messages, growing in confidence and developing his skills in message development and delivery. He effectively shepherded the flock with maturity, responsibility, and wisdom, as attested by many in the church family who said that they "watched him grow before their very eyes!"

Also, a temporary team of "advisors" had been appointed to assist Joshua during Roger's absence. Out of that group, one man in particular demonstrated biblical leadership qualities, and has since been added to the elder board.

In the strong bond of mutual love that I share with these people, I was affirmed and embraced as we returned. I appreciate that they include me as one of the sheep with no extra "pastor's wife" expectations. They have allowed me to maintain a moderately low profile with my assorted forms of service on an as-needed basis. It was clear that "absence makes the heart grow fonder."

Rhythm: What have we learned? What is the long-term benefit of sabbatical? Frequent evaluation and assessment is required to maintain balance amidst commitments and objectives and sabbatical rhythm. God ordained the Sabbath principle for our protection in the day-to-day rhythm of life; it must be guarded and practiced in order to experience His design for peaceful, purposeful, and productive lives. In the year that has passed since our sabbatical, we observe that we have remained diligent with most of our re-formed goals and that some have been allowed to lapse. We also see that when we are less faithful, there are adverse effects—thus the value of periodic assessment! We have renewed our commitment to adhere to the goals we set during sabbatical, and to re-evaluate more frequently. We remain grateful for God's ever-present help as we seek to continually trust and obey Him.

It's All About Family: Ann, Cromwell, CT

I had the privilege of participating in two sabbaticals with Howard. The first sabbatical was when we were pastoring a church in Bellevue, Washington; the second was this past year, as Howard serves in the role of a superintendent in our church denomination in New England.

My first response, as I reflect on the benefits of our sabbatical, is the profound generosity extended to our family. Sabbaticals are an opportunity to bask in the love of our Father in Heaven, demonstrated by a supportive community.

I am so grateful to those who poured love into our lives with their gifts of love.

The intensity and demands of Howard's schedule physically take him away from our family, so my children and I have always been very mindful of treasuring the time with him when he returns to us. His travel schedule prevents him from being able to commit to serving as a coach or a carpool dad, but he shares in our lives by being invested in each of us in a very supportive role.

Because of our commitment to having a healthy home life, sabbaticals are not as much about recovery as they are refreshment, deepening our connections with each other, and FUN! We have been given the opportunity to travel to places we would not have otherwise budgeted time or money for— Hawaii, a lake house by a pristine lake in Washington state, and visits to Montreal and Quebec, Canada. On our first sabbatical, people from the church in Washington state, where we served, even helped us remodel our house by donating time, tools, and expertise.

All in all, we have found our sabbaticals to be refreshing and fun, providing relaxing occasions where our focus can be on family togetherness and enjoyment of one another.

Willing, But Wilted: Cindy, Loudon, NH

"Where there's a will, there's a way." If you were to Google that phrase for a definition, you would find the name

Stephen A. Ludwick, along with his photo. He is the only man I know who can tear apart a broken car starter, a malfunctioning sewing machine, motor cycle engine, or refrigerator, and make it as good as new without a manual. When the church computer expert said the computer couldn't display the sermon image on the big screen, Steve took the challenge. The result: the computer displayed the image on the big screen and on a small monitor display at the pulpit.

He's the only man I know who pays attention to the details of people's lives, then quietly finds a way to meet their needs. When a homeowner member is away, Steve will snow-blow a walkway, keep pipes from freezing during a storm, and feed their animals for them. He sings hymns to dying family members, transports people to appointments, and visits strangers. He will stand at a hospital bedside all day, in the middle of the night—24 hours at a time, if necessary—advocating for a family, or keeping silent when there's nothing to be said. He has the uncanny way of taking on the difficult challenges or confrontations that others run from; he does this deliberately and delicately (usually) saying the hard things when needed. That man is my husband. And he is a pastor.

Over the last thirty years I have grown to depend on him and his strength. What he does for others is small in comparison to what he does for his wife and family. It amazes me how a new bottle of shampoo appears in the shower the morning after I throw away the old one, or that the daily smoothies never run out. While I work outside the home, the meals are cooked, the cars are tuned, the dogs are groomed, and the bills are paid. Then there are the days spent in our children's homes fixing plumbing, painting, rewiring, or patching holes. Do you get the picture? He literally burns himself out for others—in his own family and in the church body.

As a dedicated a pastor, Steve displays his love for the Lord by serving his family, friends, our church families and their families—practically anyone he comes in contact with. He serves by rolling up his sleeves and getting his hands dirty; he has never been very good at delegating.

Unfortunately, Steve began to avoid people back in 2010. It was subtle at first. Truthfully, I didn't realize what was happening until he finally spoke to me about it. He came home one night and told me the church board had voted for him to take a three-month sabbatical. My first response was, "Why?" In retrospect, Steve told me that his pastor friend, David Alves, had spoken about the need for sabbaticals for ministers, but it never crossed my mind that my husband actually needed one.

My understanding of a sabbatical was taking several months away, possibly overseas, to research and write a book. For all of my husband's strengths and abilities, research for writing a book is not one of them—at least not yet. That night Steve explained to me how tired and spiritually drained he was; he felt he had nothing left to give. My heart went out to him. Then I realized that he meant for me to join him on that sabbatical break! There was no way I was going to leave my home in my young adult children's hands for three months. I held my ground for a long time, trying to finagle ways for Steve to get the rest he so desperately needed and for me to stay home to preserve my job—and my home. Our God, who is so gracious to us, had a better plan.

We were scheduled to start the sabbatical on July 1, 2010. We weren't actually going to leave until July 5, after our annual church picnic and fireworks. That event became a send-off for us, a celebration of trust in the midst of unspoken concerns of what would take place over the next three months. I was amazed at the planning that was involved for the sabbatical, and the education and preparatory work that took place with our church family and us; both they and we, with our own fears and concerns, prayed for God's leading and for His provision.

The first six weeks were spent in our camper, close enough to home for me to continue work. Steve was instructed not to contact church people; they were asked not to contact him. In truth, I thought many of the written guidelines were overkill. But it didn't take long for me to understand the need for our "guidelines"; *Steve had a very difficult time letting go.*

One particular incident was over housing for a drama team that was coming one Sunday morning. Steve wanted to organize and take care of the crisis of housing them. Our daughter, who is just as strong-willed as her father, told him at that Saturday send-off to "stay out of it." It is comical now, but not so funny at the time! It took Steve about four weeks to begin to rest and unwind. At that point, I had a two-week vacation which we spent together, enjoying God's creation and each other. It was possibly the first vacation we have taken together that wasn't interrupted with telephone calls or a crisis of some kind.

When we returned from our vacation, we were to spend the last six weeks at a cabin on a lake arranged by our church association's conference president. I had forgotten that arrangement and was very content to stay in our nice camper. I pictured sparse quarters in the cabin, without many of the necessities of life for six weeks. Steve agreed that he would check the cabin out while I went back to work. He texted me to say we would be staying at the cabin; I didn't need to worry about bringing anything but our clothes. The cabin turned out to be a garage apartment at an eight-million-dollar home on Lake Winnipesauke in New Hampshire. We lived like royalty for six weeks, watching some of the most beautiful sunrises and sunsets. It was a quiet place, with every luxury imaginable. Our hosts were so gracious and sought to make our stay memorable. Writing this even now, I get overwhelmed at God's love and tender care for us. We spent time, both individually and together, nurturing our spirits, seeking God, and experiencing Him in ways we hadn't found Him before. Amazing things happened during our weeks at the cabin.

As the time for our return home approached, I admit to once again feeling some trepidation. We knew the Lord had ministered to us, but how would that play out when we returned to everyday life? Would the church still want us or had they realized they no longer needed us? Did they find someone they liked better while we were away? Would they be receptive to some of the changes we felt were necessary? Would their expectations of their pastor be met when we returned? And for me, what would my home look like when I got back?

Our home was in tip-top shape on our return, our pets were alive and well, and only the porch flower pot was among the missing. Our return was met with a Sunday of celebration and sharing of God's goodness toward us as well as to our church family. God had proven Himself to be faithful.

Steve began to preach with a renewed enthusiasm for God's Word that we hadn't seen in a long while. Since that time, we have seen the Spirit of God move in ways that leave us speechless. The Lord has changed hearts and developed each of us in ways that we never imagined.

We are back to the "everyday routine" but are now walking in a new dependence on our Lord. We have learned the importance of waiting on the Lord, allowing Him to renew our strength. Through the sabbatical period, my relationship with my Lord has grown stronger. But it didn't stop there. God has caused our relationship with each other to reach new heights.

Relationships in the church are also much stronger. Through this sabbatical period, God brought about a greater sense of community and love within our church family. Truly, when we follow the leading of our gracious, Heavenly Father, He works in ways beyond what we could ever imagine. To Him be ALL the praise and glory!

Falling in Love Again: Lisa, Pembroke, NH

My husband and I were pastors of a growing church. In 2008, we took a sabbatical from our church and from our role at that time as Northern New England District Supervisors for our denomination.

Though we both profited from the sabbatical, it was much needed by me; I found myself in a balancing act between being a wife to a high level senior leader, mother to our three teenagers, and my role as a pastor and leader to many. During the time of sabbatical, I stepped away from my responsibilities with people and drew closer to the Lord. It was during this time of personal renewal that I fell in love with the Lord again and began to see myself not as a leader, but as His daughter. This was the key benefit for me as I spent daily personal time sitting with the Lord—letting Him love on me for who I *am* to Him, and not what I *do*. So often in ministry we are pulled off in different directions and can easily forget who we are in the process. This time of sabbatical caused me to center in on who I am in the Lord.

The sabbatical was also beneficial in helping me to view my relationships with my husband and children in a different way. My eyes were opened to how much I was neglecting them. I didn't see it before, but God revealed it to me when I stepped away from church ministry. During sabbatical, my husband and I would take long drives together and found ourselves enjoying each other's company again. Neither of us would talk about ministry, and we actually found that we have a lot of other things to talk about!

At dinnertime, we laughed together as a family and we played games after, with no agenda but to enjoy each other. There were no meetings to rush off to and nothing that I had to oversee, so my family got all of my attention and it was wonderful! It was an amazing benefit to be able to enjoy family without the distractions of ministry.

One of the surprising benefits of taking a sabbatical was realizing how much our pastoral staff doesn't need us. They were able to function quite well without our oversight (imagine that!). This sabbatical caused them to step up into leadership roles and to be stretched. They all succeeded very well, which increased our confidence in and appreciation of our team of leaders. Our congregation was also very supportive of us and the other pastoral staff while we were away on sabbatical. The people were gracious to our staff and prayed for us, which was very encouraging.

All in all, our sabbatical was much-needed and beneficial to my husband, my children, our leadership team, our congregation, and . . . to me. Our church has a policy of an eight-week sabbatical for full-time staff once every 10 years. Though our denomination has no set policy, they do suggest that their churches have a sabbatical policy. I would highly recommend that every church have in place a sabbatical policy for their leaders.

Marcy's Summary

In my personal story, I revealed some of the tough things that pastors of many churches face, especially those men and women who serve in smaller churches. Pastors of mega-churches have other issues to face that I did not address in my story; I haven't walked in their shoes.

Each of the other pastors' wives and I have shared our sabbatical stories to encourage you, the body of Christ, who benefits from the sacrificial giving of the lives of your pastors and other full-time and part-time staff, to consider how to bless those ministry leaders. It would be well to do as Paul instructs: "Let the elders who rule well be considered worthy of double honor, especially those who labor in preaching and teaching. For the Scripture says, 'You shall not muzzle an ox when it treads out the grain . . .'" (1 Timothy 5:17-18).

Notice the picture of the ox and the grinding mill: the ox is working hard to make food available for others, and should, himself, be given opportunity for sustenance, rest and refreshment. Obviously the ox can't eat while treading the grain; imagine the indigestion he would get if he tried to do that. He has to be set free from the yoke for periods of time to be able to eat and get refreshed.

Your pastor and other leaders need to be periodically released from the yoke of ministry work for a time of refreshment and nourishment. You will be blessed and honored by the Lord as a church body, by honoring those who serve among you and by making provision for them to have times of ceasing for personal refreshment and rejuvenation. God bless as you as a church consider how to serve the servants of God who faithfully minister to you and your families.

5 ✦ FIVE BENEFITS OF A PASTORAL SABBATICAL FOR YOUR CHURCH

HERE ARE FIVE IMPORTANT CONSIDERATIONS as you think about how your church will benefit by loving and honoring your pastor with a ministry sabbatical.

1. You will be obeying God's Word.

In various places in Scripture, the church is admonished to consider, honor, esteem, and imitate its leaders. Christ is the Head of the church. He is the one who has placed its pastors where they are. How we treat our pastors is either aligned with Christ's purposes or it is not. When we align with what Jesus is doing in our churches, we will see fruit and blessing. Spiritual formation flourishes under His leadership. He is generous and caring about His under-shepherds. Is your church in step with what the Spirit is doing in the churches?

2. *You will have a grateful, renewed, and refreshed pastor.*

No pastor I know who has taken a ministry sabbatical has returned saying, "Well, that was a waste of time." The pastors I have talked with, without exception, have enthusiastically embraced and now champion spiritual renewal leave for other pastors. They look upon their sabbatical as a high point in their personal spiritual formation and refreshment. The only exception to this rule is a couple of pastors who related to me that they took a "mini-sabbatical." That reminds me of the saying, "Sermonettes for Christianettes." When we truncate spiritual renewal leave, it will leave us still needing spiritual renewal and a genuine ministry sabbatical. Sleeping for two hours a night when we really need seven to eight hours a night will catch up with us in short-order.

If your church prioritizes a sabbatical policy and practice, your church will have a pastor who is grateful, renewed, and energized. This can only benefit the people.

3. *You will be investing in the families of the church.*

The families of your church need to see how the pastor parents and manages his family. I believe that the pastoral family, like it or not, is displayed *intentionally* by the Lord. He wants us to learn from those who have the right (or wrong, as the case may be) priorities in their lives. I have seen churches destroyed by a pastor who did not understand this principle to put his or her immediate family first by taking time to be with them. Extended time to be with his or her own family is crucial to a healthy ministry and a healthy church.

When a church is well-taught and can see what they're being taught lived out, then they begin to understand the principles that underlie a family taking time away, together. The body learns how Sabbath rest refreshes and restores. Granted, the ideal is to live this out on a weekly basis, but sometimes it takes a sabbatical to give pastors the time and space to reprioritize and renew expended energy, and to allow others to meet their needs as they have poured into the lives of others.

4. You will ensure that your church and future leaders will be spiritually healthy.

Once the pastor and church have experienced a ministry sabbatical, they have a positive shared experience. Both have seen that a sabbatical can produce an abundance of fruit, both personal and corporate. The pastor finds that he or she can take several months away from responsibilities and know that the Lord will manage His church. This has a tendency to restore trust and confidence in Christ and His oversight of the church body. The leaders and people see that the Lord uses them to lead and assume greater responsibility. This has the effect of building confidence in those who step up to serve. They see that their gifts can be used to supplement the pastor's ministry in their midst. They become equipped by doing. They will also recognize the importance of being spiritually healthy themselves. Experiencing the pastor's sabbatical also prepares them for any unforeseen pastoral absences or emergencies.

5. *You will be better equipped and prepared for the next sabbatical.*

Having lived through one and seen its effects, the next ministry sabbatical will be easier. Now the church, the pastor, and others are better informed.

Given the overwhelming positive benefits of ministry sabbaticals, every church should proactively adopt a sabbatical policy. This is good practice and a sensible priority. In our association of churches, the five superintendents met to develop and adopt a suggested sabbatical policy for all five regions in the United States. They are encouraging all the churches in our association to develop a sabbatical policy. They know that this can only help the churches to increase pastoral and church health, and thus, flourish.

What about *your* church? Do you have such a policy? I have included a couple of examples in the resources for churches so that you will have a track to run on. For the sake of your church and pastor, I urge you to consider, adapt, and develop one of those policies to make it your own. You should find enough in this primer to assist you to make good decisions as you plan for your pastor's sabbatical—possibly the first he or she has ever taken.

Because the Holy Spirit cares about churches, He cares, too, about its pastors. You do yourselves a great service by joining with the Spirit in taking care to love and honor your pastor.

6 ✦ THE OBJECTIONS

FIRST, HERE'S MY TONGUE-IN-CHEEK CHECKLIST of the only valid reasons for your church NOT to encourage a ministry sabbatical for your pastor.

- You might have to step up and use your spiritual gifts.

- You're afraid you might have to sit in one of those fancy wooden chairs up front (traditional churches only).

- He'll have way too much downtime with his family and friends.

- She might find out that she really needed the rest.

- He might actually enjoy more intimacy with the Lord and his spouse.

- He might not stay depressed.

- God might speak to you about how you need to engage more in the ministry of your church.

- A sabbatical might slow your pastor down . . . then what?

- He could learn that it's not about he as a pastor *doing for* God, but about his *being with* Him.

- All that rest, relaxation, reading, walking, sleeping, prayer time, and travel would be hell on earth for our pastor.

- The pastor and his or her spouse might grow deeper in love by revisiting their beginnings.

- He might have to spend more time with his kids, just having FUN . . .

- Your pastor would miss his cell phone too much.

- Your pastor might forget the way to his or her office.

- What if he comes back feeling great and then you have nothing to complain about?

- She might have an experience that will involve a renewed vision that you will have to participate in.

- You might find that God honors Sabbath rest, especially a sabbatical!

I hope my attempt at humor has helped you to see more of the benefits and some of the flimsiness of our questions and concerns.

Face Your Fears

Most objections to a ministry sabbatical are fear-based. What is the church afraid of with regard to a pastoral sabbatical?

Honestly, for some churches, it's a no-brainer. They are priming the pump. They are sowing to their spiritual future. They are insuring a lasting ministry with strong foundations.

But some churches have honest fears. Let's look at a few more:

- **How will the church hold together?** Isn't Jesus the head? And aren't all the joints and ligaments held together by the head?

- **Who will preach on Sundays or lead prayer meetings?** In-house resources, creative worship services, and outside pulpit supply are all options. In this day and age, there is a plethora of resources available for local churches.

- **How will our pastor afford a sabbatical since he lives on a salary?** Where will he get his support from? Sources range from saving ahead of time in a sabbatical account to applying for grants from Christian foundations. Creativity and intentional planning will go a long way to ensure that funds are available.

- **How will we convince our pastor that he needs a sabbatical?** This comes up on occasion because some pastors remain out of touch with what their spirit and bodies need. On the other hand, it may not be as hard as you think. Get a copy of my first book, *A Sabbatical Primer for Pastors*, and give it to your pastor as a gift, or point him or her to SabbaticalPrimers.com. There are good resources there to help.

- **Once our pastor is convinced, what then?** Now you begin. Now you initiate and navigate the proposed sabbatical.

Congregational Objections to a Sabbatical

OBJECTION 1: "The members of the church hold full-time jobs and they don't get three to six months off. Why should our pastor?"

I think most people can immediately see a couple of things wrong with this mindset. First, it's extremely demeaning, in an abusive way. Is your pastor worth something to your congregation? Is ministry important enough for him or her to be at the top of his game? Why would the pastor's care be subject to worldly ignorance regarding the pastoral role and responsibilities? Do those who work in the congregation have jobs that are 24/7? Those who do should have extended leaves.

Except for a few first responders, others do not have the

24/7 pressures that pastors and their families have. Nor are they on call 24/7 in all the crises of life and seasons of change for a congregation of families. As Thom Rainer says, "Many pastors can't 'turn off' work in their mind. Even on their days off, they are waiting for that next telephone call or next crisis. Thus, they never relax."

For robbing his kingdom, Satan has targeted those leaders and their families who have forsaken all to serve on the front lines of ministry. Most church members or attenders do not experience the relentless, chronic spiritual attack and oppression that spiritual leaders endure. Unless they've been there, it's difficult even to imagine. This is especially true in certain regions of the country like New England, where witchcraft and occult activity is so prevalent and active that the Massachusetts State Police has a detective assigned specifically to occult crimes.

I didn't understand the pastor's vocation even though I tried to vicariously. I had to become a pastor to truly understand from the inside. Before that, no matter what a pastor or pastor's wife related to us in our itinerant ministry, we could see in their responses that Marcy and I didn't understand pastoral ministry.

OBJECTION 2: "We've never had a pastor who took an extended Sabbatical before—except for hospital stays."

In Barbara Gilbert's *Who Ministers to Ministers?*, one pastor laid out the following rather shocking reality of the pastoral vocation:[4]

I am appalled at what is required of me. I am supposed to move from sick-bed

to administrative meeting,

to planning,

to supervising,

to counseling,

to praying,

to trouble-shooting,

to budgeting,

to audio systems,

to meditation,

to worship preparation,

to newsletter,

to staff problems,

to mission projects,

---

[4] [The Alban Institute, Inc.-Washington, DC]

to conflict management,

to community leadership,

to study,

to funerals,

to weddings,

to preaching.

I am supposed to be "in charge" but not too much in charge,

administrative executive,

sensitive pastor,

skillful counselor,

dynamic public speaker,

spiritual guide,

politically savvy,

intellectually sophisticated.

And I am expected to be superior, or at least first rate, in all of them. I am *not* supposed to be:

depressed,

discouraged,

cynical,

angry,

or hurt.

I *am* supposed to be

upbeat,

positive,

strong,

willing,

and available.

Right now I am not filling any of these expectations very well. I think that's why I am tired.

See your pastor anywhere in that description?

It's irrational to say that just because we've never done it *that way*, that we can't change. Otherwise, how would any person or any family grow? We need to adapt and change with changing circumstances within biblical guidelines.

OBJECTION 3: "How can we afford it?"

The better question would be, "How can you *not* afford to provide your pastor and his or her family with the rest God requires?" At some point, the mindset that holds the feet to the fire is a destructive misuse of the precious stewardship God has entrusted you with in your pastoral family, your church, and in your own spiritual journey.

More and more churches, denominations, and associations are recognizing the deep needs and making provisions for pastoral sabbaticals. They can provide guidance for you and the congregation, resources for pulpit supply, and help with planning. Some denominations even have leaders serving in pastoral health or as sabbatical consultants. Those people are there to help you to help your pastoral leadership remain vital in ministry. Don't be shy. Call upon them.

The church should continue your pastor's salary while on sabbatical. Nothing has changed. The church's income should remain the same whether the pastor is there or away. If the pastor were not taking a sabbatical, the church would still be paying a pastor, right? So there's no reason the pastor cannot continue receiving whatever compensation is currently allotted, assuming the congregation has had teaching on the generous nature of their heavenly Father. In the case where pastoral income is based upon the pastor being *at the building*, then your church has deeper spiritual health issues that should be addressed alongside the pastoral sabbatical. A situation like this in our conference of churches is an opportunity to help educate and encourage the church in the pastor's absence.

Several denominations and foundations, such as The Day Foundation and Louisville Institute, provide sabbatical resources.

If you're an Advent Christian in New Hampshire or Vermont, the *Maranatha Conference* gives a generous grant to qualifying churches to help the pastoral couple attend a renewal retreat at a pastoral ministry center. On my last sabbatical, our conference helped me and my wife attend a pastoral refreshment center recommended by *Focus on the Family*. Many conferences and denominations can supply the pulpit for small churches with no staff, or those with few people qualified to bring a weekly message in the pastor's absence.

Some church associations or conferences make both people and/or funds available to help with pulpit supply. You can research them and make a list that works for your church.

OBJECTION 4: "Our church could not survive without our pastor present!"

Really? Is that a healthy condition? Isn't the church built upon Christ? Is *He* the shepherd of your church or is it your pastor that is the foundation stone? Christ alone is the Chief Shepherd. The pastor is an under-shepherd serving Christ and you. Sabbaticals are designed to minimize the congregational fear that the pastor may want to move on to another church following the sabbatical. Yet in the pastor's absence, people can step up and do things that in the past the pastor did alone. This is delegation and equipping at its best, not displacement.

It is the church's place to assure the pastor that you have no intention of replacing him or her, but that you'll be under the shepherding ministry of Jesus whether the pastor is present or on sabbatical.

OBJECTION 5: "We've never offered a ministry sabbatical before."

Right . . . so get started! Just because you've never done it before is no reason for not doing it once you realize both the reasons and benefits of a sabbatical for your pastor and for your church.

Why not join your pastor in a proactive leadership approach, leading in what is biblical, positive, and good? Ask your pastor if you could help him or her to develop a sabbatical policy. Or talk to a leader who has influence and can make it happen.

Most churches testify that they have been amazed at the results of a sabbatical. Following a pastoral sabbatical, I often hear comments like, "We've gotten back a brand new pastor. It really should be a priority for every church."

OBJECTION 6: "We're such a small church that if the pastor weren't here no one would show up."

That's a good thing to know. But I don't believe it. Not if you are a real church. God's people do not forsake the fellowshipping of themselves one with another. Even if you had to meet in a home, you'd be a house church.

As long as God's gifted people, who are being led by the Holy Spirit, can meet, they will. If they're not motivated to meet together, then you have a bigger problem than your pastor is likely to solve.

Where there's no commitment, there's no life—only a

religious shell. You're in a dysfunctional church. Better to know that right up front and ask the Lord to join you to a gathering of His people who walk with Jesus and one another in love.

But if your "small church" has a pastor who loves Jesus and you, and if the people of your church love one another, then size means nothing. God often chooses the small and insignificant to do great things with. So grant your pastor a sabbatical and *you* be the one to draw everyone together under Christ. Who knows . . . when the pastor returns, he or she will be amazed at what a sabbatical can do for a little church. Now that's worth showing up for!

7 • How to Get the Most Out of Your Pastor's Sabbatical

O KAY, I'M CONVINCED. *How do we begin?*

By deciding as a church leadership to allow and even encourage your pastor to draw closer to the Father for an extended period of time, you have made the most important first decision.

First Steps

Are you as a church in this alone? Do you have any denominational or associational officials who are knowledgeable in the sabbatical process? If you do, then contact them; let them help you get up and running. They may have specifics about your context.

For instance, in our regional association of churches (New England, New York, and Pennsylvania), pastoral health is a primary focus and priority. We have made a concerted effort to serve our fellow pastors and their churches by making sabbatical resources available as they become known to us. We also provide pulpit supply when pastors are away on sabbatical. This is a huge benefit to pastors and churches.

In our local association of churches (New Hampshire and Vermont), the *Maranatha Conference of Advent Christian Churches,* generous financial assistance is available to any of its pastors who wish to take a sabbatical. They also provide pulpit supply to any church whose pastor is on sabbatical. Our churches need only apply. In addition, the Maine Conference of Advent Christian Churches voted a couple of years ago to make books and other resources available to pastors who are interested in pastoral health and sabbatical renewal.

Sabbatical Mentors

Don't assume that your pastor knows the ins and outs of taking a sabbatical. Many pastors have never been introduced to the ministry sabbatical. This was not covered in many seminaries nor have many pastors seen it modeled by those they may know or respect. I've seen pastors take a three week break without changing much and think that they have taken a sabbatical. That's why I wrote A Sabbatical Primer for

Pastors. To get pastors up to speed on the basics of a ministry renewal leave—a sabbatical. Whether your pastor is a veteran at sabbaticals or has never taken one, encourage him or her to read the primer for pastors.

Outside sources can be extremely helpful. Conference officials can walk you through the process and share with you the resources that are in place for your church and pastor. It's great to serve with a team.

If your church doesn't have such a person or group, no problem . . . just keep reading. I write to point you in the right direction to find just what you need to initiate and navigate your sabbatical seasons. Also, I make myself available to serve churches and pastors that need suggestions or counsel with regard to sabbaticals. Your pastor or church leadership can reach me at info@sabbaticalprimers.com.

Your pastor also may be a resource for sabbatical planning and may know more about sabbaticals than he or she has communicated to you. Sometimes pastors are hesitant to champion their own cause because it seems too self-serving. So they lay low, even though they may be informed and desperately in need of a sabbatical. Find out what your pastor knows about sabbaticals. Ask if he or she has ever taken a sabbatical. Buy the pastor's primer I suggested earlier and give it to your pastor. Pastors *love* to add books to their library. It's the rare pastor who doesn't collect, read, and study books.

Once you have taken your first steps, your church then needs to get the most out of the ministry sabbatical.

Pre-Sabbatical

We encourage the pastor and the church leadership to dream, discern, design and plan for the coming sabbatical ideally two to three years prior to the sabbatical. In many cases, the need for a sabbatical becomes apparent through a crisis situation and must be executed in a much shorter timeframe. This is why each church should establish a sabbatical policy and timeline long before the actual need presents itself.

The church should go through a time of identifying and categorizing ministry resources to assist the pastor and the church in this planning stage. This pre-planning doesn't have to take a huge amount of time—perhaps just a few hours of joint prayer, sharing with one another possible sabbatical resources. Some time spent at PastorsAdvocate.com or another pastoral website would prove helpful. We also share resources for both pastors and churches at SabbaticalPrimers.com. Check in from time to time. Better yet, sign up on the website to receive emails informing you of new postings.

Your pastor also needs time to formulate a sabbatical dream and needs the freedom and time to get away before the actual sabbatical to pray through the pre-sabbatical suggestions.

Encourage your pastor to carve out some time—a couple days away—to dream, discern, and plan. Ask, "Hey, Pastor, have you set aside a dream and plan retreat for your sabbatical?" Let him or her know that you support that designated downtime. Often pastors sense that because they're "paid" staff, they are often viewed as employees who need to punch in on the clock. They may personally feel that if they take a short time away, they're not giving 100 percent. Often the congregational or leadership mindset has to change first, so that the people stop viewing your pastor as a corporate executive, but see him as a shepherd of Jesus.

When Jesus calls any of us to "Come away with me by yourselves . . ." we are not only free to go (Mark 6:31); we must go! The mindset has to change in the church environment first. An individual, elder, leader, board member, deacon, etc., can be a catalyst to begin this change of church culture in order to reflect a more biblical view of loving and honoring the pastor as you move into and through the pre-sabbatical and sabbatical policy development.

Dream

What would your church's envisioned outcome of the ministry sabbatical look like? Do you want your pastor to return with a new sense of purpose? Perhaps you're hoping for a deeper experience of the Father's love for him or her. Are you aware that for some pastors, reading the Word can become boring or rote, because they've been mining for sermon material for so long? This is more common than most pastors are willing to admit. A sabbatical presents a wonderful opportunity for a refreshed and rekindled love of God's Word. Your part is to pray that your pastor's love of the Word will be renewed daily while on sabbatical. Also, ask the Lord to plant a dream deep within the church and the leaders, including the pastoral family.

Discern

Discerning is a little different than planning. Much planning is about *our* ideas, expertise, and opinions. We trust that the Lord is the one directing those three as we form our plans. However, discerning is finding out what He's doing, what *God* is up to, and aligning ourselves to Him and His plans. By taking intentional time alone and together in His presence, we sense what He's doing and where He's going, and we *do* and *go* with Him. Jesus said that He only did what He saw the Father doing. He only spoke what He heard the Father speaking.

For years, the elders of our fellowship went away together for our "Elders' Day." We had breakfast together at a local restaurant first (we skipped breakfast at times when we had decided to fast), and then drove to a cottage by a lake owned by one of the elders. There, we usually spent the first half-hour casually enjoying being together and getting comfortable while nursing a cup of coffee or tea. Then one of us usually shared a verse of Scripture and off we went, individually, to spend the next 20 minutes alone, pondering that verse. This was followed by a period of time to write down what came to us, as we rolled the verse over in our minds and hearts. We took a short time of individual prayerful response, thanking the Father for any insights for ourselves or our church body. Next, we came back together and spent an hour or so talking about what we individually "heard." Finally, we shared any personal needs we had and prayed together for each individual elder. All this before we touched on any church "business" or congregational issues.

Following our focused time of personal ministry, we talked about any pressing issues that we discerned in our watch-care-oversight of the people in our fellowship. Without exception, we *never* came away without both hearing and receiving wisdom from God regarding our inquiries and pastoral issues (James 1:5-8). Of course, we entered these times expecting the Lord Jesus to build *His* church.

I would find it extremely challenging to serve in a church leadership that transacted "business" and used secular planning methods to get at the heart of what God is doing and communicating among His people. How can a church discern in such a worldly paradigm? The Church of Jesus

Christ needs leaders who, together, know how to discern and hear from the Lord.

We encourage your church leadership to get alone together before the Lord to discern His mind for your church and your pastor during his or her ministry renewal leave. Perhaps this could be done away from the church building or personal living space, surrounded by nature. Do any of your leaders or congregants have such a place? Perhaps they would love for you to meet there to inquire of the Lord together (Jeremiah 10:21). Or you could rent a space from a local Christian conference or retreat center. Midweek, many conference centers would love to host you and it does not interfere with their weekend retreat schedules. Whoever gives you space, give them a generous gift as demonstration of your appreciation, love, and support for their ministry.

When you're together, turn the cell phones off, and leave them off. Unless you're on a top-secret assignment, and the President of the United States may need to communicate immediately with you, the messages really can wait! I've lived over half a century without texting or email, and though I appreciate these technologies, we really can live without them for a few hours—often more peacefully and clearly focused in the present moment. Nothing is more rude than to see a leader take a call in a meeting or not know how to turn of the ringer when a call comes. What's being done in your face to face meeting as leaders takes top priority. The only exception should be if Jesus wants to get ahold of you—and He won't use a cell phone to do it.

Find a comfortable, secluded place to sit away from distraction. Corporately and individually embrace your Father's presence. We tend to be far too impatient. Slow down! Give the Holy Spirit time to penetrate your head and your heart, then see how He meets you. His promise is that when you're still, He will reveal himself in ways that will amaze you.

"Be still, and know that I am God. I will be exalted among the nations, I will be exalted in the earth!" The LORD of hosts is with us; the God of Jacob is our fortress. Selah. (Psalm 46:10–11, ESV)

Perhaps He'll give you specifics (James 1:5); perhaps you'll receive a leading or sense of something related to your church's or pastor's needs as you consider together the pastor's sabbatical. Westerners tend to compartmentalize time segments. Most of us move through our day with our To-do list. "We did this, now we're done. We did that, now we're done." Pay attention to what ensues in the hours following your time with the Lord. Don't be too quick to close out the time and move on. Let your time linger in your heart and mind.

Share what you receive, together and individually. Discuss your leadings and impressions together. Then commit your group discernment to prayer. Defer to one another in love. The Lord will surprise and delight you.

We need less planning and more discerning—seeing and hearing what the Lord would have for us, His church, and the upcoming sabbatical. Keep a balance in all things; the best, most effective planning derives from discernment.

Design

I've made a list of several design items that could be helpful at this season of sabbatical planning.

1. Develop a proposed sabbatical policy for the church.

Church leaders need to press ahead to develop a Sabbatical policy for the church to follow, for both present and future pastors and/or pastoral staff. If you really want to be generous, you could include other staff as well if you're a larger multi-staffed church.

Find out if your denomination or association has a sabbatical policy. If so, you may want to adopt it outright or adapt it.

Engage the pastor in drafting the policy. Your pastor may know where to find resources. He or she may have served a previous church which had an established policy in place. If not, then have him or her refer to my book *A Sabbatical Primer for Pastors*. As I become aware of them, I will be sharing some sabbatical policies on the websites at both

SabbaticalPrimers.com and PastorsAdvocate.com.

In conjunction with your church and/or spiritual leadership community, along with your pastor's input, finalize your church's sabbatical policy. After following the steps necessary for approval of church policies, you can put the policy into effect according to the timetable you all agree upon.

Once you adopt a policy, please send me a copy at info@sabbaticalprimers.com, along with permission to post in online to help other churches looking for sample policies.

2. Be sure to answer such questions as:

- How often should a sabbatical be granted?

- What will be the terms of service regarding this time away? Who will fill the gaps, such as Sunday messages, visitation, Bible studies, prayer meetings, emergency contact persons, etc.?

- Who will act as the contact person for outside pulpit supply: engaging the speakers and seeing to their travel costs, honorarium and hospitality when they come to speak?

- What financial preparations will the fellowship and pastor make? In addition to the suggested financial preparations, you may want to consider applying for sabbatical grants or funds that may be available to your pastor or the church through your denomination or association or a para-church organization or foundation. Many exist. (As you locate them, please send me links which I can make available to other churches.) The church should consider budget items for:

- o Continuing the pastor's salary while he or she is on sabbatical

- o Helping with travel costs and cost of retreats geared to spiritual formation and ministry to pastors, as part of their sabbatical

- o Pulpit supply

- o Perhaps your fellowship or church would consider setting aside $50 to $100 per month as a line item called a "Pastoral Renewal Fund" or "Sabbatical Renewal Fund" for the years leading up to the sabbatical. Then, by the time the sabbatical comes, there will be money accrued toward the sabbatical without adding an overwhelming strain onto the sabbatical year's budget or resources. How much the church should put aside can depend upon many factors. The amount the church should save ahead should be in accordance with what is needed in order to provide your pastor with an effective sabbatical and to continue his or her compensation while he or she is away.

- Should we have Pastor's Advocates?

  ○ Pastor's Advocates is a ministry developed by the Superintendent of the Eastern Region of our association of churches and embraced by those of us who have had a lead role in pastoral health. Pastor's Advocates has been recognized as a unique and helpful ministry. This is where documents found at PastorsAdvocate.com can be of real help to you. There, under the menu button "Advocates," we are adding resources as they become available; there you can find out more about the ministry of Pastor's Advocates and read some of the newsletters that have gone out to Pastor's Advocates in the Eastern Region.

  ○ Include a clause in your new policy regarding "Pastor's Advocates" if your church is establishing this new ministry to your pastor.

  ○ You should answer the following questions:

    - How many Advocates will we have?
    - Who will serve?
    - How will they be chosen? Will they be appointed by the pastor or volunteered? The pastor should have the greater say in how his

or her advocates are selected.

- What will be their role at your church?
- What will their ministry look like?
- What role will they have as it relates to your sabbatical policy?

Putting these things in place will be a great legacy of your pastor's ministry and of your church leadership, not only for your current pastor's spiritual health and formation, but also for the pastors and leaders who follow him or her. If you're not sure what to include or how to begin, make use of the resources I've made available. (For this section, you can specifically refer to "Sabbatical Policy Samples" at Sabbaticalprimers.com as we make them available.)

3. If your church has provided a previous sabbatical, review your notes and memories.

See if there's anything you'll need to change this time around. What really worked for your church? Was there a speaker that the church especially appreciated? Perhaps you'll want to invite that speaker back as your church schedules pulpit supply for the sabbatical.

Would you add something that you feel was missing? Did you factor in enough time for preparation with the pastor? Make sure your pastor makes a list of things you'll want to cover in his or her absence.

4. If you've never offered a pastoral sabbatical, talk to someone who has.

Contact a church leader from another congregation and find out what worked well for them. Read articles by pastors or churches who've shared their sabbatical experiences.

5. Consider what you would like to do as a church body.

Perhaps you'd like to launch the pastoral sabbatical with a special celebration or at some other regular church event; include a send-off prayer for the pastoral couple or family. It's never too early to schedule and plan the event. Family Bible Church in Loudon, New Hampshire combined their annual Fourth of July fireworks celebration with the sabbatical send-off of their pastoral couple. It was memorable for all involved.

Maybe you'd like to provide a weekend at a special place for the pastoral couple. You may want to book that accommodation and begin to save toward that expense as a church.

Finally, as a church, lay out some general goals and preferred outcomes for the sabbatical.

6. Consider what you should NOT do as a church body.

This can be as important as what you will do. You should not communicate with the pastor or pastoral family while on sabbatical (except in agreed upon or prearranged circumstances such as family or church emergency, death or acute illness of a person in the church, good news, etc.)

Beginning early in your dreaming, discerning, and designing will not only be wise; it will encourage your leadership to anticipate your pastor's sabbatical rather than fear it or be caught off guard.

One Year Prior

Your pastor will likely be spending a little time each month getting more specific in his or her plan. Your church leadership can do the same. From time to time, one of the leaders may want to speak to the congregation to prepare them as well. You could even use a message on some of the texts I've shared in Chapter Three or from Pastor Mark's letter in "Resources for Churches" at the back of this book. Every week, share one of the testimonies from the pastor's spouses section of the primer in Chapter Four.

Sabbatical Launch

You are ready to launch your pastor out on sabbatical. The church or leadership has approved it. Your pastor has agreed and together you've put it on the calendar. You have made sure that everything's in place for him or her to confidently begin the sabbatical experience.

Expect trouble or interference at this point. If it doesn't come, great! But be prepared for it. It's part of spiritual warfare (Ephesians 6:10ff). Nothing worth something comes easy. And if something can happen to prevent your church from follow-through, it might happen at this point. Make sure you have people praying all the way along the planning process. This can ward off problems the week before or a few days before your pastor begins the sabbatical. Organize a team of volunteer intercessors to pray specifically for the pastor's sabbatical and for the church during his or her time away. Here's where Pastor's Advocates can be a great help. They can serve on such a team and/or lead a prayer effort.

As you enter the sabbatical, make your watchword "freedom." Allow the pastor to be free from all demands. Communicate clearly to the congregation that the pastor is not to be contacted. Share with members contact information for one of the staff or someone from the leadership community.

While your pastor is away, consider what tasks might be draining his or her energies. Plan ways to form a working team on his return. As folks in your church step up to the plate, they will grow in experience and confidence in their own ministry gifts and interests.

Cease the "shoulds": he should do this or she should do that. Extend to the pastor complete freedom from performing duties or accomplishing tasks. This is especially important for those churches that have a pastor who is performance-driven or is a perfectionist, and finds it difficult to delegate. Some are afraid that if they attempt to delegate, the response might be, "That's what we *pay you* for."

Immature or new believers are not aware that the five-fold ministry offices (including "pastor") are God-gifted and God-assigned to the church to prepare *the people* to do the work of ministry (Ephesians 4:11 and following). Pastors were never expected by Jesus, the Head of the Church, to do all the work themselves. I've known some *pastors* who needed to be reminded of their assignment to equip, too. Give your church leadership the same freedom during the pastoral sabbatical. Don't "should" on them!

The Lord doesn't drive us; He leads us. If memory serves me well, the only time He "makes us" do something is to make us "lie down in green pastures" (Psalm 23:2). Sounds like rest to me.

Jesus shepherds us; the enemy drives us.

The enemy of our soul wants us to make bricks without straw; he demands the impossible. God is taking us out of the brick-making business. Hopefully this sabbatical can do the same for a pastor who tends to be task-oriented, like Martha in Scripture, rather than relational and willing to simply *be,* like Mary who sat at the feet of Jesus listening.

What will our pastor be *doing* during this time? Little, I hope!

What follows is the plan I made for our six-month sabbatical in 2010. I include it to give you some insight into another pastor's sabbatical. As you can see, it is a very general plan. I did this intentionally because my mentor once told me that I over-plan everything. Part of a sabbatical should include a new attitude. For those of us who over-plan, we need to loosen up and allow for spontaneity, which further allows for serendipity. We need to retire our agendas and relax to let the Lord surprise us. What's the worst thing that could happen if I wake up one morning with no plan and just sit and look at my beautiful wife, an aesthetic experience from my point of view?

One quiet morning at breakfast, Marcy said gently, "What have you planned for today?"

"Nothing," I said. "What would you like to do?"

"Float together on the inner tubes and just talk."

And I said, "Hey, I never would have thought of that. Good plan."

Our time floating together is one of the most memorable times we had on our sabbatical. If the family cottage hadn't been sold several years back, we would still float on the lake on days off. But what a precious memory we have. We laughed, vented about the people we love-no-matter-what, imagined, and at times just enjoyed the quiet without any words at all.

I took a week's vacation leading up to month one. This gave me time to get our personal house in order and to pack and tie up loose ends regarding travel or accommodations, communications with friends, family or vendors. The next day, we were officially on sabbatical.

Month One—March

Week One: Home; total rest; no agenda; sit and stare; tend a garden; wash the car; do whatever gives me a sense of quiet, rest, and closure; decompress

Week Two: Visit friends; read

Week Three: Home

Week Four/Five: Easton lake house; read, contemplate, walk and dream together

Month Two—April

Week One: Home; review my "Life Mission Statement" (I suggest to pastors that if they haven't already done so, they should develop a "Life Mission Statement." It has been an invaluable resource to me when I'm considering my use of time, planning, and trying to remember what I've felt the Lord wanted me focused on.)

Week Two: Home and Easton lake house with Marcy

Week Three: Easton lake house; journaling

Week Four: Easton lake house; reading

Month Three—May

Week One: Home

Week Two: Pack and leave for New Jersey vacation

Week Three/Four: Vacation in Ocean City, New Jersey with family

Month Four—June

Week One: Home

Week Two: Pack and prep for pastoral renewal retreat at Sonscape Retreat Center in Divide, Colorado

Week Three: Pastoral renewal retreat; drive to Texas to visit friends for vacation

Week Four: Home

Month Five—July

Week One: Camp Beebe, Quebec

Week Two/Three: Home

Week Four: Home; Easton lake house

Month Six—August (re-entry month)

Week One: Motorcycle around New Hampshire together; make some decisions from what we've heard and learned

Week Two: Visit friends in New Hampshire at Alton Bay Christian Conference Center; read

Week Three: Reflect upon the sabbatical in my journal; rework my "Ministry Timeline"

Week Four: Home; ready our household for ministry again

Ministry Re-entry

This is one of the most crucial phases of your pastor's sabbatical for both your pastor and your church. This is the part of the sabbatical that you'd be most likely to downplay or ignore, without some encouragement to the contrary. If you're not careful here, your church could squander most of what your pastor has gained while away on sabbatical.

Believe me, I understand. I blew off this phase on return from my first sabbatical in 2002, a three-month sabbatical. I came back to the church renewed and refreshed, so I thought I could just jump right back into the schedule I had before I left.

You mean the schedule that got you into trouble in the first place?!

Apparently I didn't get the message, because I started running the same race I had run before. I know that the apostle Paul said he was running the race for the prize; however, he was running a godly race—a race given to him by God—and I was running a performance race given to me by the church's "needs" and my own expectations. I had not made the kinds of decisions and changes that would conserve the lessons learned on sabbatical.

God hasn't called pastors to run the performance race. We are not to serve and run like a hamster in a cage. He's called us to serve His body by doing what He's asked us to do. And we can't do that if we're exhausted all the time.

As Wayne Cordeiro said, we can't do ministry if we're "running on empty." That's why it's essential when pastors return from sabbatical, that they re-enter correctly, carefully and wisely; we encourage this by changes we as a church have made.

I suggest three priorities of re-entry. I adapted these priorities from the Oklahoma Department of Corrections' "Prisoner Re-entry Initiatives." What? We're considering re-entry based upon priorities of prisoners? Yes. Exactly. Many of us are prisoners of our schedules, our expectations, our unhealthy presuppositions, and our "invincible pastor" mystique. Once pastors are no longer locked up after their sabbatical, they will re-enter with a new mindset and some new behaviors. We need to make sure that we as local church leaders and members have transitioned ourselves to do things a bit differently.

1. Systems Check

Does the church need to change the way it as a community approaches ministry and values? Can we help lift some of the pastoral load? How will we partner to help our pastor maintain the sense of renewal and refreshment he gained from sabbatical?

Encourage your pastor to prioritize and take a weekly Sabbath—a day of sabbatical rest. No one contacts him or her. This day is a day where the church gives the pastor permission to do nothing and accomplish nothing that would normally be on a "to-do" list. This is not the pastor's day off. That needs to be a different day—a day of errands and household responsibilities. What you're offering your pastor is the same "pay" for one less day's work (assuming your pastor already has a six-day work-week). Your pastor's new five-day work week will be an investment with great dividends for the church. Studies show that when more time is given for down-time during a week, productivity is greatly multiplied. Businesses are just now catching on to this. Churches should have been teaching and modeling this all along.

Let your pastor choose her Sabbath day. Your Sabbath may be a Sunday, but typically your pastor's weekend is stuffed.

Marcy and I set Monday as our Sabbath. And since

September of 2010 we have observed it faithfully with few exceptions. I have ordered my ministry week around that Sabbath rest. I have noticed that I can work harder the other days because of the rest I take. This was God's original intent, not only for pastors but for everybody—you included. It is not a legalistic Sabbath observance, but rather a day of delight and refreshment. And God gave a promise He has never rescinded: "You will ride on the heights of the earth..." (Isaiah 58:1-4).

We lost a Sabbath observance when it became a legalistic observance rather than a day of delight and a treasure. Our culture does not give permission for people to rest and we are paying the price as a society that has been ripped from its peace, creativity, and unity.

Marcy and I stepped out of the rat-race, raging river mindset, and have, over these years of Sabbath enjoyment, established a sense of peace, calm, creativity, well-being, and healing. When people step into our home, they often comment on the sense of serenity that usually fills it. Like all people, we experience exceptions (holiday parties, celebration Sundays, sudden emergencies), but they are not the rule.

We encourage each of you to designate one day a week as a Sabbath to enjoy your walk with your Father. If married, hopefully you will agree together about a day that you'll both observe as your one day in seven of Sabbath rest. Be yeast in the lives of those you love and in your congregation. Join with your pastor and set the pace—a slower one.[5]

Be counter-culture and revolutionary in this performance-based society. Let others see that in *your* life you get things done, but getting them done is not what drives you. Abundant living will be yours. And as this is established in your pastor, and in you, it will become Sabbath yeast to transform your church culture.

2. Reflection

Reflection is crucial to conserve and reinforce spiritual gains from your pastor's sabbatical. If you skip this, then you may lose much of what your church has gained in the months your pastor has been away.

Over and over in Scripture, God calls His people to remember, to think back and recall all that He has done for them. We are forgetful (and the older we get, the more this seems to be a given). We need reminders.

---

[5] I came across a book entitled, *Slow Church*. I haven't read it so can't recommend it. But I love the title and intent and hope to read it soon.

- What has your church learned in the pastor's absence?

- Have you taken time to analyze how you navigated the sabbatical at home while the pastor has navigated his time away?

Take some time during your pastor's sabbatical to discuss as a leadership team what gains the church has made in the pastor's absence, even if it's just renewed appreciation for your pastor's ministry and family. Also consider:

- What lessons have you learned?

- Whose ministries or skills have blossomed?

- What would you do differently next time?

- What worked and what didn't?

Make notes and put them in a sabbatical planning file. You will find this helpful in planning the next sabbatical.

3. New Patterns

Hopefully you pastor's sabbatical time will result in some new patterns for both him and the church body. Consider the following:

- Encourage the practice of a Sabbath Day—as just mentioned—for your pastor and congregants; many believers count Sunday as their Sabbath, but that's a workday for pastors.

- Consider and encourage your pastor's family time and

proper rest. Don't call the pastor after 7 p.m. unless it's an emergency that can't wait until morning.

- Allow your pastor early morning hours to spend time with the Father getting his guidance and marching orders. Urge the congregation to establish such a pattern in their own lives.

- Encourage member-to-member ministry. The pastor should not bear the full burden of prayer and counsel. Sometimes all a troubled person needs is an attentive, listening ear and godly wisdom.

- Remember that the church survived while your pastor was on sabbatical. Many of the sabbatical processes implemented could stay in place, with possible modifications, after he or she returns.

- Encourage your pastor to minister in his or her areas of strengths, passions, and gifting. We all have areas that are weak and areas that are strong—yes, even pastors. Cut him or her some slack in areas of weakness. For example, my areas of strength are teaching and preaching the Word. I'm not a good administrator. My most productive hours are daytime hours—especially mornings. If your pastor is like me, doing administrative tasks depletes his energy. Study in the Word, teaching and coaching people, and writing energizes me. Find people who can supplement your pastor's weak areas so that the ministry is balanced. What can you do to help him or her in a weak area?

- If someone or several people in the congregation prove to do well in presenting a Sunday sermon or message, consider having them occasionally share a message to give your pastor a short break (assuming the pastor would encourage others to share in that ministry).

- By all means, conserve the excellent gains from the church and pastor have received from the sabbatical.

4. Mentoring

The biblical model for disciple-making is mentoring. You can call it mentoring or coaching or whatever best describes the actual relationship. We are to be godly examples as we follow and learn from the lives of other godly examples. Paul's leadership mentoring practice is found in 2 Timothy: "...and what you have heard from me in the presence of many witnesses entrust to faithful men who will be able to teach others also" (2 Timothy 2:2).

Jesus practiced mentoring as well. He even knew what size group would be practical for effective mentoring. He chose 12 men with whom to walk out His life and ministry. He also had an inner circle of three from that group.

As your pastor re-enters your church community, ask him or her about mentoring. Ask yourself:

- *Does the pastor have a spiritual mentor?* Ask him or her that question. Everyone needs encouragement from those who have walked a similar path.

- Am I being a spiritual mentor?

- How can I find and engage someone to walk with me as a mentor?

- Who should I be encouraging in a mentoring relationship?

The best book I've ever read on this topic is *Spiritual Mentoring: A Guide for Seeking and Giving Direction* by Keith R. Anderson and Randy D. Reese. Most aspects of spiritual mentoring will be found in this excellent resource on being a spiritual friend, listener, mentoree or mentor. Perhaps your pastor will mentor you in some of the insights he's received while away on sabbatical. Maybe you can agree together to live a sabbatical life.

FINAL THOUGHTS

B Y WAY OF REMINDER, EPHESIANS states that Christ, the Head of the Church, gives gifts "of men" (and women) to the church for her building-up and equipping (Ephesians. 4:8, 11-12). Your pastor holds one of the five offices in the body of Christ that makes him or her God's gift to the church. Our Father wants you to be a catalyst for your pastor to enjoy ministry wherever He assigned him or her (Hebrews 13:17b). Taking care of your pastor's spiritual health, continuing to foster his or her spiritual growth, and providing rest and renewal for his or her physical body will insure a healthy long-term pastorate. Churches grow and thrive under long-term pastorates. God blesses churches that so honor Him and His appointed pastors.

Ask the Lord what He thinks. Encourage your pastor to get

some time alone. Don't assume that God is pleased with a hurried, restless ministry performance. I feel free to caution you to guard your pastor from burning the candle at both ends because I've been there—twice. Apparently, I'm one of those who, in the past, has had to learn the hard way. But I finally got it. Now I'm modeling a way of life that many in the fellowship I pastor are imitating (Hebrews 13:7). They, and others with whom I have some influence, set aside regular time away to be alone with God. I hope you will, too. That would encourage your pastor. I know personally that pastors love to see their people excel them.

One of the men I mentor took me out in the woods and down to the river where he sets up his camp chair and sits with the Lord. He is the one who also sets up my "tent of meeting" out in our back field. This brother loves to be with the Father. He watches the river flow quietly by and listens to the birds and feels the breeze. There in the quiet, he is renewed and refreshed. He often returns from those times by the river with new inspiration for serving or insights from the Word. You can see why I asked him to serve as one of my Pastor's Advocates. His devotion encourages me. How about you?

I hope you'll see *your* need for time alone with Jesus and *Abba* more quickly than I saw mine. I hope you love and value that time enough that you won't hesitate to initiate a ministry sabbatical for your pastor so that following hard work, he or she can enter a season of spiritual renewal and refreshment.

May the Lord bless you as you use this primer to God's glory and your pastor's and church's health.

Be a Blessing to Others

Every one of you reading this book has influence in your circle of influence. If this book has served you, would you please share the product link with others who might be open to your recommendation? You can also write a short review on Amazon to encourage others to purchase and read the book. You may be used by God to bless another church or pastor. You will certainly be blessing me and Marcy.

Bookmark the website PastorsAdvocate.com and share it with your pastor and others. Prayerfully consider being a pastor's advocate.

Drop by my author page on Facebook and "Like" it so you'll get updates.

The Lord Jesus bless you as you bless and refresh your shepherd(s). Drop Marcy and/or me a line at info@sabbaticalprimers.com and tell us how this book served you, your church, and/or your pastor.

RESOURCES FOR CHURCHES

The following section contains materials you may find helpful as you research and consider how you will speak to the church regarding the ministry sabbatical for your pastor(s).

Pastor Mark's Letter

BEFORE WE LEAVE THE topic of how a sabbatical can benefit your church, let's hear from Pastor Mark Bickford.

A couple of years ago, serving as the President of the *Maranatha Conference of Advent Christian Churches,* Mark wrote a letter to the conference churches in New Hampshire and Vermont. You will not only find it informative, but a good summation of what has been shared in this primer. I published portions of it below with his permission.

For the first 30 years of my life as a Christian and church member, I scoffed at the idea of pastoral burnout. It seemed to me that a pastor's life was one of ease. After all, he only worked one day a week and that was only for a half-day. How difficult could it be? Then God called me to pastoral work and I realized how totally wrong I had been.

I have since developed a much greater appreciation for the overall workload and stresses placed on a pastor's life and the life of his family.

As you read this letter, there might be some skeptical looks and raised eyebrows. One of the primary goals of the *Maranatha Conference* is to promote church health. Generally, healthy churches are led by healthy pastors. Our pastors are not a disposable asset. Several churches in the conference are declining and others are struggling just to maintain what they have. Relatively few are growing and healthy. Not coincidentally, there are several pastors who are either burnt out or rapidly getting there. Let me share some statistics concerning North American Churches.

The American Church:

- Churchgoers expect their pastors to juggle an average of 16 major tasks
- Pastors who work fewer than 50 hours per week are 35% more likely to be terminated
- 87% of Protestant churches have full-time pastors
- 76% of all congregations in the US are either plateauing or declining
- The typical pastor reaches a level of greatest impact on a church after five years
- The average pastor lasts less than five years

Pastors:

- 1,500 pastors leave ministry every month due to moral failure, spiritual burnout or contention in their churches; of those who leave for moral failure, follow-up indicates they were exhibiting signs of spiritual burnout long before the moral failure

- 50% of pastors' marriages will end in divorce
- 80% of pastors and 87% of their spouses feel unqualified and discouraged in their roles
- 50% of pastors are so discouraged that they would leave ministry if they could, but because of their specific training and calling, they have no other means to make a living
- 80% of Seminary and Bible school graduates who enter the ministry will leave the ministry within the first five years
- 70% of pastors constantly fight depression
- 70% say the only time they spend studying the Word of God is when they are preparing a sermon
- 80% do not have a close friend or confidant, nor do they time to develop one

Pastors' Spouses

- 80% of pastor's spouses feel their spouse is overworked
- 80% wish their spouse would change to another profession
- Over half say the most destructive event to occur in their marriage and family was the day they entered the ministry
- 80% of pastors' wives do not have one woman that they would consider as a close friend in the

church their husband pastors

As you can see from the statistics above, many of our pastors and their wives feel isolated and ineffective. What solutions are available to encourage and support our pastors?

And on the seventh day God finished His work that He had done, and he rested on the seventh day from all His work that He had done. (Genesis 2:2)

For six years you shall sow your land and gather in its yield, but the seventh year you shall let it rest and lie fallow, that the poor of your people may eat; and when they leave the beast of the field may eat. You shall do likewise with your vineyard and with your olive orchard. Six days you shall do your work, but on the seventh day you shall rest; that your ox and your donkey may have rest; and the son of your servant woman and the alien may be refreshed. (Exodus 23:10-12)

Come to me, all you who labor and are heavy laden, and I will give you rest. (Matthew 11:28)

For the Son of Man is Lord of the Sabbath. (Matthew 12:8)

So then, there remains a Sabbath rest for the people of God, for whoever has entered God's rest has also rested from his works as God did from His. (Hebrews 4:9-10)

When and where do our pastors find their Sabbath rest? The expectations placed on them by congregations and the expectations they place on themselves place great demands on their time and energy. Most pastors are on call 24/7 for whatever emergencies may arise. They are expected to have the correct answer in all of life's situations and to serve as mediators to all types of disputes. They are expected to provide council and support to all those in need but to never need it themselves.

I spoke with a pastor who lost two children when they were swept off a bridge during a torrential downpour. At the time, his wife was giving birth to another child. The whole church gathered to offer her comfort and support. The expectations were that he would find his comfort in God and would, in fact, comfort the congregation. He was, after all, the pastor and should be able to handle this better than anyone. It wasn't until a group of elderly women—prayer warriors—came to his home and offered him comfort and prayer that he was free to become a grieving father.

It is important that we remember how very human our pastors are and that we allow them space to rest in God and be spiritually, physically and emotionally restored. This is a level of refreshment and restoration that is not attainable in a family vacation. It is only attainable by a Sabbath rest. Your pastor is not likely to ask you for it, but allowing your pastor to become trapped in a cycle that continually drains their resources until they literally have nothing left does not benefit them or your church. The reaction of many churches when they see their pastors at this point is to replace them. Both the pastor and the church they serve would benefit from a time of sabbatical rest.

The *Maranatha Advent Christian Conference* ministerial committee would like to encourage the churches in the conference to establish a sabbatical policy for their churches. If the pastor has been with you for an extended period of time, we would encourage you to give them a sabbatical during this calendar year. Then develop a policy that would allow for continual refreshment periods during their pastorate. If, for example, your pastor had been with you seven years or more, without a sabbatical, we would recommend that you provide him with a minimum of a three-month sabbatical. We ask that you continue to support your pastor financially during this sabbatical.

Recognizing that most churches have not planned for this event, the *Maranatha Conference* desires to minimize any additional financial burden on the churches. The conference is willing to supply the pulpits of those churches that would need it in the absence of their pastor. Other financial considerations may be available on a case by case basis and needs are made known to us by the churches. We recognize that each church is unique and our goal is to respond to your specific challenges, needs, and circumstances.

Several good books are available on the subject of

burnout. Three that have proven helpful to others in the conference include *Battling Burnout* by Bill Mills, *Leading on Empty* by Wayne Cordeiro, and *How to Keep the Pastor You Love* by Jane Rubietta.

Blessings!

I realize that Mark's letter was rather lengthy, but you can see why I included it in its entirety. Mark's heart for pastors and churches is evident. I know that he would agree with me that if this letter can somehow plant a seed or encourage action on the part of church leaders to provide a sabbatical and develop a sabbatical policy for the church, it will yield fruit far beyond Mark's initial hopes when he wrote the letter to our conference.

Sample Brochure Given to Congregation

Sample Contents of Brochure Given to the Congregation from the Leadership

The content of this brochure was created by one of the pastors of the Maranatha Conference for his church to introduce the congregation to the call for a ministry sabbatical. (*Published here with permission.*)

A Call for

Pastoral Sabbatical

Rest and Renewal

2010

Church Name

Location

Pastor's Name

Pastor's Tenure [optional]

SABBATH-KEEPING

What is a Sabbatical or Pastoral Spiritual Renewal?

First of all, the word "sabbatical" comes from the biblical word, Sabbath. The keeping of the Sabbath originates in God Himself. "By the seventh day God had finished the work He had been doing; so on the seventh day he rested from all His work. And God blessed the seventh day and made it holy, because on it He rested from all the work of creating that He had done" (Genesis 2:2-3).

The word Sabbath means "to cease" or "to rest." The Bible instructs us on three Sabbath-keeping practices:

❖ The **Sabbath Day** ordained as a weekly observance set aside solely for the cessation of work in order to renew people in body, mind and spirit.

❖ The **Sabbath Year** to occur every seven years when all crop-bearing land would be allowed to lie fallow so the earth could rest and be replenished for future harvests.

❖ The **Year of Jubilee** to be celebrated every 50 years with no harvest or rent but instead, debt forgiveness, restoration and the making of offerings.

So the keeping of Sabbath—ceasing and resting, renewing and refilling—are part of the Judeo-Christian rhythm of work and play, of production and reflection, of giving out and taking in.

CEASING AND RESTING

What does spiritual renewal look like for your pastor?

A sabbatical rest will be a time to disengage gears from 21 years of Pastoral ministry at [church name] to cease from the usual routine of sermon preparation and preaching, meetings, counseling, giving advice, weddings and funerals, the administration of day-to-day church affairs and the daily shepherding of people.

It is a time for:

- A complete break from ministry at [church name]
- Rest, reflection, evaluation and some travel
- Quality time with family
- Attention to unfinished personal projects
- Getting recharged by quality time in God's Word and other inspirational reading.
- Renewed focus and vision for [church name]
- Dreaming dreams and receiving visions

It is NOT considered to be a time of:

- Extended vacation
- Sick leave
- Focusing on negative aspects of ministry.
- Doing things that distract from the central purpose of rest and renewal.

How long will the pastor be gone from [church name]?

The plan is for the three months of July, August and September 2010 with a return the first week of October.

Will [pastor's spouse's name here] be joining the pastor?

Some of the time, yes—however, [name] will continue to have a work schedule, except for her two weeks of vacation. She will be with him on weekends and will be taking a break from leading worship on Sundays.

RENEWING AND REFILLING

What are Pastor's goals for this time?

✓ To get away, disconnect and rest from ministry at [church name] for a period of time

✓ To go to another level of intentional spiritual formation through reading, prayer and seeking spiritual direction

✓ To consider what expanded ministry might look like for [church name]

✓ Organizing thoughts concerning ministry and personal priorities

✓ To explore leadership models that might give [church name] a better handle on moving forward with the vision Jesus is revealing to us

✓ Perhaps take in a Pastoral Retreat or Seminar if available and if funds permit

FREQUENTLY ASKED QUESTIONS

Where did this idea come from?

Our *Maranatha Advent Christian Conference* is encouraging churches to provide times of Sabbatical rest and renewal for pastors who have 7+ years in one church. The recommendation was discussed and unanimously approved by the Church Official Board.

Why now?

The Lord has brought this to our attention at this time and we do not want our pastor to reach the point of personal burnout. We believe this time is overdue for him to take an extended break from the stresses of pastoral ministry after 21 years of ministry here. This will allow him to be undistracted in seeking personal and spiritual renewal that he might return strengthened to continue to lead [church name] into God's greater blessing that is ahead of us.

Who will cover Pastor's responsibilities?

[Name] is a credentialed minister within our denomination and will carry the lead responsibility for preaching and day-to-day pastoral care of the church. [Name] will continue his ministry activities as usual in collaboration with [church leader's name].

The *Maranatha Advent Christian Conference* will provide

additional ministers for preaching when [pastor's name] is unavailable. The Conference President has agreed to be a resource and is available if necessary.

Will [church name] be in a "holding pattern" while Pastor is away?

All of our ministries will continue as usual while [pastor's name] is away, and perhaps even new ones will begin! It is important to remember that the Pastoral Spiritual Renewal is a two-way process: while Pastor is on his journey of sabbatical rest, renewal, and reflection, [church name] will embark on a journey as well—embracing the occasion for our own reflection and renewed focus on God's call to be His Body and continue to discern God's will for the [church name].

Will Pastor be in contact with us while he is on his Pastoral Spiritual Renewal?

An important part of this process is for Pastor to make a complete break from the things that he does day in and day out. The only persons who are to contact him will be [church leader's name] and Conference President, Mark Bickford. In the event of some extraordinary event that must absolutely be communicated to Pastor [name], Elder [name] will take care of contacting him.

Who will pay for the Pastoral Spiritual Renewal?

Pastor's weekly salary will continue as normal to support his regular family budget. However, there will be extra expenses related to his sabbatical for travel, lodging, seminars, books and the like for which donations will be gratefully accepted. The *Maranatha Conference* has volunteered to help with some of these expenses along with compensating those who provide pulpit supply.

Sample Pastoral Renewal Proposal

Submitted by David C. Alves to the Leadership at New Life Fellowship

This was to be reviewed by our leadership and then submitted to a foundation for a grant. This was for my first sabbatical in 2002.

Pastoral Renewal Proposal

PART A

Summary Statement

In His relationship to His disciples, Jesus often took them aside to "be with Him."

Situation 1 - Mark 6:31-32

31 Then, because so many people were coming and going that they did not even have a chance to eat, he said to them, "**Come with me by yourselves to a quiet place and get some rest.**" 32 So they went away by themselves in a boat to a solitary place.

Situation 2—Luke 9:10 (NIV)

10 When the apostles returned, **they reported to Jesus** what they had done. Then he took them with him and **they withdrew by themselves** to a town called **Bethsaida** ("a town situated probably at the northeast corner of the Sea of Galilee near where the Jordan River flows into it.") [6]

---

[6] Achtemier, Paul J., Th.D., *Harper's Bible Dictionary*, (San

With this as a background, I propose the following focus for my sabbatical:

REST IN A QUIET PLACE BY THE WATER: Contemplative

Refreshment and revitalization involve the physical, mental, spiritual, and emotional. The prime directive would be to get away and rest with the Lord. I need a restful season, just enjoying Marcy and some time by the water. Lake Wallenpaupack in Pennsylvania is where we have regularly stepped out of our busyness for the past 22 years.

We have often withdrawn there to refocus, pray, and listen for the Lord's direction. Much of our ministry has been impacted by our time together there. Our place at the lake is one of the constants in our life of inescapable change.

REFLECTION: Renewal and Reading

The second and fourth month, I would prayerfully read and study. The second month would include a leadership renewal event of some sort either in North Carolina or Colorado.

WRITING: Expressive

I have kept a journal for over 24 years. The third month, I would journal the sabbatical and make various entries available to the congregation through email to our leaders. These could be shared at appropriate times during the week. This serves several purposes. First, it would keep me disciplined in my reflection. Second, the congregation, through a weekly update, would know how Marcy and I were doing so that they could better pray for us.

I would also make use of reading reports. I normally write a report on each book that I read so that the content is not lost to me. My strategy would be to master several books and to skim several others related to my writing and teaching. My focus for reading would be mainly limited to the areas of spirituality, communication and

---

Francisco: Harper and Row, Publishers, Inc.) 1985.

leadership.

For the third month, I have been drooling at the possibility of getting launched on one of three needed projects:

- *New Life Fellowship College of Ministry Mission Statement and Course Syllabi:* This would fulfill God's call on both me and our church to raise up leaders for the harvest here at home. We would propose a partnership with the current regional initiatives and try to work out a practical training curriculum in cell church transitioning and church health skills.

- *Book or Workbook:* Working title: *God's Favorite Name*—from which I will teach, preach, and encourage a passion for God and for growth in character.

- *Engaged Couples' Retreat:* Coordinate a retreat aimed at young adults who are planning to marry or want to prepare for that future possibility.

I would need to pray about which project should take priority. I invite your input to know which one *you* think would be the best stewardship of your gift of time to me.

Proposed Activities:

Month One—May 2002—Rest and Review

- Weeks 1–2: Decompression / Preparation for R&R (home and local; open cottage)
- Weeks 3–4: Myrtle Beach, South Carolina or Lake (prayer and walk by the sea; reflection with Marcy on past years of ministry; BCC board meeting; read journals)

Month Two—June 2002—Refreshment and Reading

- Weeks 1–3: Israel / England trip

Month Three—July 2002—Writing and Reflection with Marcy at the Lake

- Week 1: Reading, reflection, and journaling
- Weeks 2–4: Writing and project

Month Four—August 2002—Re-entry

159

- Week 1: Open or continued writing
- Week 2: Complete project (to be determined)
- Weeks 3–4: Hospitality with fellowship families at lake, Vermont or home

Rationale

Recently, our leaders agreed that Marcy and I should apply for this renewal program. They did so knowing that this opportunity to participate in an extended time of reflection, restoration, refreshment, and contemplation would benefit both the congregation and us.

We, as a leadership, agreed that without the grant our church could not afford the expenses for our time away. The leaders have shared this opportunity and concern with the congregation. Having received an initial favorable response from the covenant members to continue to pursue the "Clergy Renewal Program," we are submitting the paperwork. We feel that time away for me and Marcy to enjoy the Lord, reflect on our ministry, and invest in our marriage can only strengthen our serve here at New Life.

The leaders are willing to step up to the plate and make it happen. I am fond of the concept that leadership arises to the occasion when we pastors lead by example then move out of the way to allow them to develop their gifts. I know that the leadership we have has enough trust-credibility with the congregation to move the congregation through these four months that we would be away. Otherwise, I would not even consider being away. As a result, this will give me the confidence to step away and really enjoy the Lord and my wife so that we can return for many more years of fruitful service in discovering and training leaders at New Life Fellowship.

My wife and I have served the Lord both in itinerant and pastoral ministry for 24 years. In those 24 years, we have never had a sabbatical. We have been with this church for six years. When we heard about your program from one of our elders, we felt that perhaps this might be our opportunity to get aside with Jesus together. Whenever Marcy and I have taken breaks from ministry, we have returned refreshed and renewed. Our only regret was that our vacations never seemed long enough. It always seemed that we were just getting rested when we had to return to the work. We inevitably agreed how wonderful it would be to have more time—both to rest and to write (we both write and Marcy speaks nationally and internationally).

The timing works well since we have just made an upward turn in our qualitative and quantitative growth. We are growing healthier and seeing a great opportunity to spread the ministry between emerging, qualified leaders. I have four men who have just completed Phase I of our Regional Lay-Pastor Training. They will have completed Phase II by the time we leave for our sabbatical. We have almost a year to complete our Lifegroup Leader training scheduled for the fall and to launch one or two Alpha groups from those who complete the training. I would still have half a year to resource those leaders before we would be stepping away.

All in all, this concept could not have been brought to our attention at a better time for both the congregation and my family. We only hope that we fit your requirements and that the Lord agrees.

PART B

Congregational Information

1. New Life Fellowship is 14 years old, founded in 1987. The church is a replant of the original 100-year-old Advent Christian Church of Concord, New Hampshire.
2. We have approximately 65 in attendance on Sundays with 80% of those being Covenant Members. Of our total Sunday attendance, 100% are in cells or small groups. Our qualitative growth and health is excellent.
3. New Life Fellowship pastors:
   - 1987—1995: Bruce Jones
   - 1996—present: Dr. David C. Alves
4. NLF is not a program-based church. We are a cell church patterned off of the book of Acts. Most of the ministry flows from the lives of our cells. For us, this is the most biblical means for fostering the quality of Christian community assumed in the New Testament. The needs of the congregation are met through the daily lives of these basic Christian communities. On occasion the Lord does raise up gifted individuals to carry out jail ministry or some other such outreach, but they are dependent on gift-based

ministry.

5. See attached documentation for IRS information.

PART C

Pastoral Information

1. Education
   - Asbury College—B.S. 1982
   - Gordon-Conwell Theological Seminary—M. Div. 1988
   - Regent University—D.Min. 2000
2. Ministry Timeline and Ordination
   - 1981—present: Co-founder and Director of Frontline Ministries, Inc.
   - 1987—1994: First Baptist Newburyport, Massachusetts; Pastor of Youth and Families, and Specialized Ministry
   - 1988: Ordained American Baptist 1st Baptist Newburyport, Massachusetts
   - 1994—1996: New Hope Christian Fellowship Sutton, Massachusetts (planted)
   - 1996: Maranatha Conference of Advent Christian churches recognizes and accepts 1988 ordination
   - 1996—present: New Life Fellowship Concord, New Hampshire
3. Pastor is also the Director of Church Health and Planting for the *Maranatha Conference of Advent Christian Churches* of New Hampshire, Vermont, and eastern New York. In this capacity he coaches and mentors several other pastors and their churches. He also teaches regional training courses. He has served as the U.S. presenter for Advanced Cell Training to pastors' conferences and is a certified consultant for *Natural Church Development*.

Program Budgets

Month One—May 2002

- Week 1: $1,150
- Weeks 2—3: Ocean City, NJ; $3,500
- Week 4: Read journals at Phil's; $200

Month Two—June 2002

- Weeks 1—2: Leadership Retreat; $2,500
- Weeks 3—4: Reflective reading; $500

Month Three—July 2002

- Week 1: Tour continued OR research begins
- Week 2: Research (GCTS); $300
- Weeks 3—4: Writing; $1,500

Month Four—August 2002

- Week 1: $500
- Weeks 2—3: $400
- Week 4: $150

Total Budget: $10,700

"Sabbatical: The Missing Link for Churches and Pastors"

By Dr. David C Alves

First Printed in the Advent Christian *Witness, Winter 2012*

Has anyone noticed the toll that modern ministry is taking on our pastors? Pastoral fatigue and burnout is costing the church more than money; it's costing lives. More pastors and leaders are leaving ministry today than in the history of the Christian Church. I know because I almost became one of the statistics.

About two years ago, I began to experience depression for no particular reason. I felt discouraged, defeated, depressed, and doubtful things could get much better. I began to withdraw from people. Small tasks seemed huge. Everything took so much mental and physical energy that I didn't know how I could continue in the ministry.

Follow that with a TIA (mini-stroke). Add to that my wife's cancer. Then imagine the church beginning to decline. If anything negative could happen, it did.

Fortunately, at the recommendation of my doctor and in response to my health needs church elders granted me a 6-month Sabbatical.

My story has a happy ending. Our sabbatical did great things for Marcy and me. We returned to ministry refreshed, re-inspired, ready to serve as though we had just begun ministry. I recovered the strength and stamina to re-enter with new priorities in place and a replenished store of serotonin.

Read carefully the following text:

He gives power to the faint, and to him who has no might he increases strength. Even youths shall faint and be weary, and young men shall fall exhausted; but **they who wait for the Lord** *shall renew their strength; they shall mount up with wings like eagles; they shall run and not be weary; they shall walk and not faint. (Isaiah 40:29–31, ESV)*

The Holy Spirit through the Prophet Isaiah said that *even the youths and young men* will be weary and fall. How much more the older men and women? Notice the answer? They who WAIT upon the Lord. Linger with the Lord. Take time to be with Him. They shall renew, mount up, run, and walk unhindered. That's the kind of pastor or leader I would want to lead me, to model life for me.

Most churches don't have any idea what's happening to their pastors as years of people-ministry and spiritual warfare take their toll. So when their shepherds "burn out," many churches simply replace the pastor with another pastor and before long find that he too needs replacing. Is that God's plan for those gifted people He gives to the body of Christ to build it up? Is that the future He has ordained for churches--a constant stream of committees on the search to replace tired and hurt servants?

Let's take a closer look in part 2.

How many pastors are leaving the ministry annually?

Info from <u>Focus on the Family, Ministries Today, Charisma Magazine, TNT Ministries</u>, and other respected groups [reported at http://djchuang.com] found:

- **1,500** pastors leave the ministry permanently **each month** in America. [emphasis mine]
- **7,000 churches close each year in America**. Reported from <http://djchuang.com/2010/churches-closing-and-pastors-leaving/>
- **90%** of the minister's report they feel inadequately trained to meet the demands of the ministry, 70% report having a lower self-image now than when they first started and **50% of the ministers will not even last 5 years!**

Pasted   from

<http://pastoralcareinc.com/MR/Books/EBooks.php>

These figures are staggering. Perhaps one or two or twenty pastors may have neglected their spiritual life in order to be there for everyone else. Or perhaps they have misplaced priorities, but 1,500 a month!? Fifty percent of ministers will not make it past 5 years? WOW!

What are the blockbuster-issues affecting pastors today?

I believe that the following factors contribute directly or indirectly to the statistics which we've just read.

--a decline in respect and appreciation.

According to one survey, the occupation of pastor ranks near the bottom of the most-respected professions, just above "car salesman."

Reported   from: <http://pastoralcareinc.com/MR/Books/EBooks.php>

Some congregations view their pastors as hired employees or hired hands. Such a view is simply unbiblical and dishonoring to Christ, who gives pastors to the church.

As one source said, "the congregation wrongly believes that it is the pastor's job to evangelize the community and pull the strays back in."

Reported from: <http://djchuang.com/2010/churches-closing-and-pastors-leaving/>

In reality, according to Ephesians, pastors hold one of the five-fold offices in the church. Theirs is a calling, a vocation, and they are not expendable. They are gifts to the Bride from Jesus himself. They are to be honored and valued.

--long hours and "battle fatigue" leading to exhaustion

Some in the church believe that a leader walking in the Holy Spirit, and in dependence upon Jesus, will never tire or be worn out. Of course this view is short-sighted and ill-informed. But these super-spiritual church members apply simplistic answers to complex conditions. Then they err again by plucking biblical verses out of context without taking into account the whole counsel of Scripture.

They really have no idea the intensity of spiritual warfare and burden many pastoral couples labor under. Some pastoral leaders don't even recognize the source of their distress.

Focus on the Family's resident Pastor's pastor, H.B. London, said recently:

"Many well-meaning Christians in their congregations ignored the signs of "battle fatigue." Instead, congregations overwhelmed my pastor friends with unrealistic expectations, negative criticism and misplaced anger. Some congregations even assumed the perfect pastor was "out there," so their fallible pastor was terminated."

http://www.parsonage.org/faq/A000000541.cfm

Is termination a valid choice for our war-weary troops on the battle front in Afghanistan or Iraq? Those who have withstood the frontal assaults in battle are moved for a time to the rear to recover and retool before redeploying again to the front. Why would we expose those who watch over our souls to years of intense ministry without much more than a few weeks of vacation a year? School teachers get the entire summer off annually. Pastors, elders, and other spiritual leaders operating in modern culture are under so much more than their predecessors of earlier times. But even in those earlier times, spiritual fatigue and exhaustion took its toll.

Jesus knew what it was to be weary. The Apostle Paul understood the weight of ministry and spiritual concern--compassion fatigue is real. Exhaustion is the body responding to the load of spiritual warfare and pastoral care. God constructed our bodies for a slower pace than modern life dishes out.

--low pay

Have you ever considered whether you could go through years of preparation for ministry, years of schooling and graduate studies (if a M.Div. is required for ordination as it is in most denominations) and survive on what the average local church pays its pastor?

It is estimated that about 75% of all ministers live close to the poverty level. . . Many expect the pastor and his/her family to have a *higher* set of standards than they [themselves] do and unfortunately, having [sic]to "live by faith" more in providing for their provision.

Reported   from:

<http://pastoralcareinc.com/MR/Books/EBooks.php>

Pastors are intentionally and unintentionally kept poor. Very few at the same level of education, experience, and responsibility would work for what the pastor receives. And once the pastor's effectiveness has been drained, the church simply replaces the pastoral family without much more thought, never mind a substantial severance package. Some church goers feel that the pastor who buys into the modern ideas of 401K's, severance packages, and housing allowances is unspiritual. These folks argue that the early apostles and Jesus didn't have any of these things so why should their pastor? But how many of them hold that same standard for themselves?

Perhaps we reap in our lives <u>spiritually</u> what we sow into our leaders' lives <u>financially</u> (cf. 1 Cor. 9:14; Gal. 6.6; 1 Tim. 5.17-18; esp. Lk. 6:38). Greediness is never applauded by God. Nor is it one of his attributes. Generosity and a giving spirit is what He demonstrates and expects from us, especially toward those men and women whom God has given to the churches. We are never rewarded for keeping our leaders poor.

What can we do to stem the tide?

--understand the nature of ministry

Ministry is like no other job on the face of the planet. Why? Because it's not a job! It's a vocation--a calling. God gives to the church gifts of men (Eph. 4.11ff). These people-gifts who hold offices in the body of Christ carry weights like no other vocation. Period.

What kinds of consideration and compensation should a person receive who:

o   Is on call 24/7.
o   Is the front line for personal tragedy
o   Sees the worst and best of life. Has to bury a child in the morning and be joyful with the newlyweds in the afternoon.
o   Has to study and prepare teaching and messages to equip God's people
o   Has to protect his family and flock from the spiritual attacks of a supernatural being set upon destroying and ravishing men,

women, and children.
o   Walk point against that enemy himself

--demonstrate Appreciation

One solution proposed by *Focus on the Family* is a congregation's annual participation in <u>Clergy Appreciation Month</u>, and a habit of affirmation throughout the year.

Pasted from <<u>http://www.parsonage.org/faq/A000000541.cfm</u>>

We just came through annual Pastor Appreciation Month--October. What did you or your church do to demonstrate how much you value the life and love of your pastor(s)? Showing your love in a tangible way honors Christ and your pastoral leaders.

--a Sabbatical

A sabbatical can be the missing link for your church and your pastor. God meant for us to rest from our labor. The sabbatical is not just for church leaders anymore, but it certainly should be practiced by our churches and leaders.

Many resources abound in our age of books, internet, and information. These suggestions may prove helpful:

☐   Simply Google "sabbatical" and see what you come up with.
☐   Assign someone from the church to thoroughly research what's available. Beginning with this issue of <u>The Witness,</u> begin to read about how a sabbatical might just meet the needs of your church and leaders.
☐   Read some of the suggested materials found at the end of this article
☐   Go to the <u>Maranatha Website/Blog</u> and see what you can find there. We're always adding sabbatical resources.

--a policy of refueling.

"Come Away: Jesus Calls His Sent Ones to Time Alone With Him."

Even Jesus recognized this and retired <u>often</u> to places in the wilderness or to fishing with friends. He valued and modeled rest and solitude.

Churches can realize that pastors need time to refuel and replenish. Then develop a policy.

Answer questions like:

☐ How often should we send our pastor on sabbatical? [some say every 5 years, others every 7]

☐ How long should a sabbatical be? [in most cases, 3-6 months is sufficient. Any may be time away, but is NOT a sabbatical]

☐ What resources will we contribute? What other resources are available?

☐ What are our plans for our pastoral staff as they near retirement age? What is that age to be in our church and culture? Is retirement mandatory at our church or is it indefinite? Are we willing to lighten the load of aging pastors rather than relegate them to an old age home (assuming they can afford one)

☐ What would honor Jesus in the way we honor our leadership?

--release pastors to fulfill Christ's expectations, not ours.

The pastor is God's called, anointed gift to equip the church. Forget this, and you can forget Kingdom effectiveness. You may have a thriving, huge church, but it has no authority or lasting Kingdom fruit unless Jesus has assigned the leaders. The pastor/elder is not an employee of an organization--easily replaceable by calling the seminary or bible college. Where would the church have gone to get a Paul or a Barnabus? What would the job description and pay have been? Who would have evaluated their ministries? Who would have presumed to give them their marching orders and told them what was expected of them? Ridiculous! Yet the church (as an organization) has lost its moorings and has the wrong-headed notion that the Pastor is the manager of the company.

Perhaps requiring pastors to fulfill <u>our</u> varied and often misinformed expectations instead of Christ's is another reason so many churches are failing and closing across <u>all</u> denominations and among other associations.

How effective are sabbaticals for pastors?

That depends upon <u>three</u> factors:

1. **Are the pastor & church committed to God's perspective of Sabbath rest?** Some pastors will have to be convinced that they need a sabbatical, especially those who are extreme people-pleasers and Type A's who push themselves and everyone around them. They need to be loved enough to be held accountable by those who love them.

2. **Are the pastor & church properly prepared?** Unless BOTH pastor and church prepare and plan, the sabbatical will not be effective. It could even be a waste of time, money, and resources. The pastor must prepare. The fellowship must prepare.
   a. Pre-sabbatical planning
   b. Post-sabbatical celebration

   Because these differ for church and pastor, I have split them in two books available online at Amazon.com and other booksellers. The titles are "A Sabbatical Primer for the Church" and "A Sabbatical Primer for the Pastor."

3. **Are the pastor & church in agreement about the terms?**
   a. Is the length of time adequate for replenishment and refreshment?
   b. Will everyone involved help the pastor to not be in the loop while on sabbatical? Calling in to see how the recent board meeting went is NOT being faithful to the trust of the church. Nor is informing the pastor that Mr. Jones decided to quit because the pastor went on sabbatical. Other leadership (local, conference, or regional) can be called upon and can handle church issues in the pastor's absence.

CONCLUSION

The problem facing churches and pastors in the 21st Century is complex and widespread, but the solution is simple. If you read and act upon the content of this article, it will positively impact you for increased Kingdom effectiveness and spiritual longevity. By caring for the shepherds, you care for yourselves. <u>Healthy pastors lead healthy churches.</u> By embracing the value of "Sabbath," both pastors and churches will fulfill their callings, honor Christ, and leave a legacy worthy of God.

[SIDEBAR]

Related Reading:

- <u>10 Reasons Why Pastors Leave the Ministry</u>, by Jim Fuller <<u>http://pastoralcareinc.com/MR/Books/EBooks.php</u>>
- Pastor's Lifeline statistics: <u>http://maranathalife.com/lifeline/stats.htm</u>
- Michael Hyatt's post, <u>Should You Dare to Take a Sabbatical?</u> / <u>http://michaelhyatt.com/should-you-dare-to-think-about-a-sabbatical.html</u>
- <u>*Leading On Empty*</u>, Wayne Cordeiro. Bethany House, 2009. Must reading. <u>http://www.amazon.com/Leading-Empty-Refilling-Renewing-Passion/dp/0764203509</u>
- David's Place, <u>"Solitude, Silence, and Simplicity"</u> / <u>http://davidcalves.com/2011/03/07/solitude-silence-and-simplicity/</u>
- <u>*A Sabbatical Primer for Pastors: How to Initiate and Navigate a Spiritual Renewal Leave*</u>, by David C. Alves

A Ministry of Pastoral Health: My Testimony

Marcy Devers received Christ as her Lord and Savior as a young teenager growing up in Franconia, Virginia. She was discipled under the ministry *Youth for Christ* in the northern Virginia area. She grew in Christ in a local Baptist church. Her life was marked by a love for God's Word, music, and the desire to know Christ and make Him known.

I came to know Jesus at age 26, through a supernatural encounter with Christ and a direct revelation of His deep love for me. He immediately became, for me, Lord and Savior. He has held me close in His love for over 36 years (and longer if you consider His care for me as an orphan).

Marcy and I met shortly after I began my walk with Jesus and together we learned about the Father's love and our sonship.

For more than 17 years, my wife and I traveled in music ministry nationally and internationally before we entered the pastorate for another 18 years. I can't begin to tell you at how many churches, camps, and conferences we've ministered across those 36 years of ministry. While in those places, many times we stayed (from one to several nights) with either the pastors of those churches or the directors of those camps and conference centers.

For whatever reason (and I suspect God was at work), pastoral couples felt free to talk to us about their struggles, or heartaches and joys of ministry. Few pastors we met had even *one* close friend. Many were embroiled in intense spiritual warfare with very little training on how to navigate those conflicts.

At some point, Marcy and I recognized that Christian leaders had a deep need that was rarely being met. Many of these servants of the body of Christ felt isolated, rejected, overworked, under-appreciated, sometimes disrespected, and second class. Some were out of touch with their need for Sabbath rest. Others were not being loved enough to have someone advocate for them to receive Sabbath rest. The crucial rest Jesus had modeled for His disciples was being denied to these mostly selfless servants. Weariness and chronic discouragement had worn them down.

Some were under severe spiritual attack. Granted some were there as a result of poor choices, but they all had the heart to serve Christ and the ministries they were assigned to.

For example, one pastor's wife was treated at a mental hospital as the result of an innocent visit to the wrong place. We later had the opportunity to piece the experience together and stand in the gap for her and the pastor for her deliverance and healing. The pastor became a serious student of spiritual warfare and learned from his costly indiscretion that demonic power was very real.

Even though we had talked with hundreds of leaders, read

many books, and served in ministry ourselves, Marcy and I realized that we only understood *vicariously* what our pastor friends were experiencing day in and day out, year in and year out. Total exhaustion plagued a majority of them. They spent themselves in the care and nurture of others while their own spiritual needs often went unmet.

At that time, the national average for length of stay in a church by its pastor was three years. Imagine, every three years the church got a new pastor. I'm sure some of that was the pastor moving on to greener pastures. But a huge majority of the transitions were initiated by the church or the denomination. When the church had enough of a pastor, or hit a conflict, they simply switched him out for a new pastor. This, of course, is also a fulfillment of the prophetic Word of the Apostle Paul who said that in the last days people would gather around the leaders who would speak only what they wanted to hear (2 Timothy 4.3). The comfortable and conflict-prone congregation also chewed pastoral families up, which is still often the case.

Enough

We had seen enough. Marcy and I sought the Lord specifically as to how we might be a blessing to those in pastoral and conference ministry. This took place in the early days of God's raising up of ministry caregivers. He began to give us insights and to lead us to passages of Scripture that underscored or confirmed desires He was placing in our own hearts for pastors and leaders.

One of the problems that we saw over and over in pastoral homes was poor time management coupled with an American cultural performance mentality. Pastors, feeling the need to be everything to everyone all the time, ran themselves crazy—in some cases to the neglect of their families. This produce-or-you're-not-worth-your-pay mentality seemed to drive many. When we asked questions about their time off, away from ministry, they often made it clear that in this modern world, there is no time off. We saw the glaring discrepancy between their ministries and the ministry of Jesus.

Even in the thick of ministry, Jesus said to His disciples, "Come away with me by yourselves to a quiet place and get some rest" (Mark 6:31). And again He said, "Come to me, all you who are weary and burdened and I will give you REST" (Matthew 1:28, emphasis mine). Even though the disciples often did not rest, it was Jesus' explicit intent. That was His expressed will for them.

We wanted to refresh and encourage those who needed it so badly. We wanted to help them get away with Jesus, to spend time with Him relaxing, being refreshed physically, mentally, emotionally, and especially spiritually. We wanted to make a space and time for weary pastors and their spouses to meet with Jesus.

Taking Action

First, we opened our tiny, three-story apartment in a New England seaport to a weary Christian camp director, and later to tired ministry couples and families. Since we were on the road a lot, our home was often empty. So we invited individuals and pastoral couples to come and enjoy Newburyport, using our apartment as their home base. We left a key and told them were they could find it. We stocked the refrigerator and freezer. We left a list of local places of interest and shared where they could find our favorite coffee shop. And they made themselves at home, enjoying three to five days of rest.

The results surprised us. They were so blessed to have that space and time to rest at no expense to themselves beyond food and travel. It touched them that our food was also available to them. Their gratefulness humbled us. What a joy to see the blessing our home and hospitality brought them. So overwhelming was the encouragement to them, and us, that we took our next step.

We wanted a larger place, but didn't have the funds to buy the estate or location we envisioned. We even chose the name well before the name became culturally popular as a result of the "Lord of the Rings" books and movies—*Rivendell*. We had read Tolkien's trilogy in the late '70's. As in the book,

Rivendell would be a place of healing, rest, refreshment and refuge from the spiritual battle. We tried to raise funds for our vision, but not much came in.

Then, my friend and mentor said, "Why not use existing facilities? Many camps and conferences are filled on the weekend and empty during the week. It could be a mutual blessing for you to develop a program that would make use of existing facilities and offer refreshment and encouragement to pastoral leaders by means of a Monday through Thursday session."

Thus began our "Come Away" weeks for pastoral leaders and church staffs. God significantly impacted the lives of leaders and church staffs through our "Come Away" weeks. We did this for several years until we could no longer afford to do it, but it gave us great experience by listening to and enabling leaders to carve out a season of rest in the midst of incessant ministry demands.

I had a gnawing conviction that we really hadn't yet grasped what many pastoral leaders were going through. We still lacked hands-on pastoral experience, so I prayerfully responded to the call of God to serve for a season as a pastor. The board of directors of our ministry, *Frontline Ministries, Inc.*, agreed with me that three to five years would give us some sense of pastoral ministry from the inside. That would position us to better understand and empathize with the spiritual and emotional exhaustion most pastors faced in their local ministries on the frontlines.

Beginning Our Pastoral Ministry

Marcy and I launched out into pastoral ministry in 1994, a year after we conducted a Bible study in Sutton, Massachusetts. The work rapidly grew into a cell church called New Hope Christian Fellowship. I was invited to be its first pastor. We worked hard to be a community and a family of believers journeying with Christ. We experienced challenges, but learned much together, and many came to Christ in a short time.

After three years there, we answered the call to New Life Fellowship in Concord, New Hampshire. Today, I still serve as pastor to the New Life family. In 2015, it will be 19 years at New Life for a grand total of 20 years of pastoral ministry, 16 to 18 more years than we had initially planned we would need in order to personally experience the challenges of pastoral ministry. And I'm still learning.

I continued to grow and learn ministry from the inside out. I've experienced every facet of pastoral ministry in small churches. Today, New Life is a house fellowship, walking where the Holy Spirit leads. We're relearning the challenges of that ministry as well.

My graduate studies centered on cell church leadership, church health, and renewal. I learned that healthy churches are pastored by healthy leaders. So as I served our church conference in the late 1990's, I helped hammer out a vision statement and to create a new position—Director of Church Health and Planting. As the first person to serve in that ministry, I made it my priority to come alongside pastors that were interested in growing healthier churches. After serving for five or so years in that capacity, I stepped out of that role in obedience to the Lord and I served in other capacities in our association of Advent Christian churches.

I continued to be under the weight of ongoing spiritual warfare for both the local ministry and the associational responsibilities that came from serving as a board member of Berkshire Christian College and as a member of the International Missions Advisory Council (IMAC) for our Director of World Missions at the time.

I tasted my first sabbatical experience in 2002, following 25 years of combined pastoral and itinerant ministry. Even though I had only been with New Life for five years, the elders and church recognized our 25 years of previous service and gave me a sabbatical of two months, combined with my regular month of vacation. I remain very grateful to my fellow leaders and the congregation for their generosity to me and Marcy back then.

So, I had three months to rest, regroup, lick wounds from a previous difficult church split, read, evaluate, regroup, and reenergize. Marcy and I made the most of our time. But I had no real guideline as to how to navigate a sabbatical. It was mostly guesswork—trial and error.

We did some things right. We traveled to England, and when we got home we traveled in the U.S. We spent significant time at Marcy's mom's cottage in the Poconos reading and writing. We understood that we had to avoid ministry in order to rest. But we did some things incorrectly, too.

I didn't realize how much my writing project would take out of me, especially because I was working on a memoir of healing. The writing and exploration of my past brought up lots of "stuff" that needed to be healed. As a result, by the time I completed my sabbatical, I was only mildly refreshed. I still felt the exhaustion of dealing with childhood memories, other issues, and the pressures of writing deadlines. I ultimately put the book I was working on aside and didn't really get back to it until just a little over a year ago.

We also didn't change our pace upon re-entry to pastoral ministry. When we got back, we were more refreshed than when we left, but we didn't put things in place that would help us to minister from a place of effective flow.

We served another eight years before our next sabbatical. During those years, I found a slight increase in focus and energy for the first five of those eight years. But in 2008, I had decidedly less to give. Of course, I was aging, too, but I knew I needed to get alone for an extended time with the Lord. Something seemed out of sorts.

I went through what I've come to describe as a spiritual winter. John of the cross called it a "dark night of the soul." He wrote a book of the same title. Nothing satisfied. All I could do was hold onto the Lord for dear life. I did not want to crash and burn as I had seen so many pastors do, usually through either illicit affairs or an addiction to pornography. While I was still free from serious temptation in those areas, I wanted to remain so. I knew I needed to do something, though. I had my own unspoken areas of struggle and only God's grace kept me from sin.

Ministry Becomes Overwhelming

So I talked with the elders and my primary care physician. All agreed. And Marcy and I took a six-month sabbatical.

This time, we did not travel as much. We stayed at the lakeside home of one of the elders for the first month and went to the ocean for a time. In June, we attended a pastoral couples retreat in the mountains of Colorado. At the *Sonscape* retreat center (recommended to us by *Focus on the Family*). Our suite had a window wall with a grand view of the nearby forest and distant 14,000-foot, snow-covered Pike's Peak in all its worship-provoking grandeur. We had a group session every morning with seven other ministry couples. We enjoyed seven life-changing days there.

At *Sonscape,* together we shared the ups and downs of various ministry contexts, beholding snow-covered Pike's Peak in all its grandeur. Again, we were impressed that we were not the only ones experiencing the daily grind and erosion of stamina that came with pastoral ministry. And our God was more awesome than the mountain we beheld for the week of our stay at *Sonscape.*

We then traveled to Texas to visit friends and see Larry McMurtry's book stores in Archer City, TX. Then returned home and took short stays in Easton at the lake house, at Alton Bay Christian Conference Center, and with friends and family over the following two months. That sabbatical refreshed and renewed us, convincing us of the absolute necessity for pastoral couples to experience an *extended* Sabbath rest—a ministry sabbatical. Marcy and I also began our own weekly Sabbath Day of ceasing—together which continues to this day with few exceptions.

Upon re-entering my ministry, I assumed the responsibility of Director of Church Health. After two years serving in that capacity, the new Eastern Regional Superintendent, Greg Twitchell, invited me to pray about joining his ERA Team as the Regional Team Leader of Pastoral Health. I prayed, sought the Lord, and invited feedback from close friends and family.

Today, I'm writing and enjoying ministry with my wife of 36 years. We still have challenges; some are severe. Marcy has dealt with stage three breast cancer that was very aggressive. We're now experiencing God's healing in answer to the promises and "words" He shared with Marcy at the beginning of the battle over seven years ago. She is doing very well at this time (except for some chronic joint pain). We are in the palm of His hand and resting in the knowledge that our Father knows what we need.

Our ministry to pastors and their families continues and we hope will expand before our mission is complete.

May we finish stronger than we started and may we demonstrate to those who know us, the life and ministry of Jesus. This has been our burning passion and single heart's desire since we came to know Him and continue to walk together with Him.

Thank you for reading this primer. May *you* too finish stronger than you started.

ABOUT THE AUTHORS

David C. Alves has served in pastoral ministry for 25 years and in itinerant ministry for 12. He graduated from Asbury  University (B.S Ed), Gordon-Conwell Theological Seminary (M.Div.) and Regent University (D.Min.). He is the author of *A Sabbatical Primer for Pastors: How to Initiate and Navigate a Spiritual Renewal Leave*; *We're the 'sons of God'...So What?: Believe God About Who You* Really *Are!* and the life-changing Amish outreach booklets, "Back to the Old Ways: A Call to My Amish Neighbors" and "Rumspringa" (youth and parent versions). He writes posts at his blog at davidcalves.com and is a guest blogger at PastorsAdvocate.com.

Together, David and his wife Marcy write and speak at leadership, spiritual formation, and couples' retreats. David enjoys his tent of meeting, old libraries, riding his motorcycle, photography, flight and air traffic control-simming, sailing, and writing in the mountains and by the water.

Visit David's blog at: http://davidcalves.com/

Marcy Devers Alves has served with David in pastoral ministry. She is a speaker, singer, (her albums are available on iTunes) and inspirational writer. Marcy is also a book editor for paupakpress.

She enjoys outdoor activities, including cross-country skiing, hiking, sailing, tennis, working in my garden, and walking by the ocean.

Visit her blog at: http://marcyda.wordpress.com/

Her blog, "Marcy's Walk" is available as a Kindle subscription at Amazon.com [click below]:

MINISTRY CONTACT INFORMATION

Consider me a fellow traveler along the path of pastoral renewal and a two-time sabbatical alumnus.

If you or your church would like me to come, I speak at churches, conferences, and schools interdenominationally and internationally. I encourage pastors and church leaderships interested in pastoral renewal, spiritual disciplines, and sabbaticals. Feel free to write me at info@sabbaticalprimers.com.

ACKNOWLEDGEMENTS

We thank all those pastors and churches that are beginning to make a ministry sabbatical a priority. Also, we thank the pastors and church leaders who read the primer for pastors and suggested we write one for the church.

We thank all those who helped bring this book to you by assisting us along the writing process:

Pastor **Steve and Cindy Ludwick** for their generosity toward us. Steve parked the 5th wheel RV lakeside at _Maranatha Ministries'_ Grace Cottage in New Durham, NH where I completed the final edits of the primer. What a wonderful blessing!

Chris and Brenda Edmunds of _Camp Maranatha_ for not only the space to park the RV, but for the inspiring discussions and home-grown tomatoes you shared with us from your garden.

The pastor's spouses who contributed _Chapter Four_ of the primer. They would include **Lisa Bonanno, Katherine Story Brown, Anne Burgoyne**, and **Cindy Ludwick**. You all made this book that much better and helpful by your honest and transparent stories.

Thanks to **Jamie Murray** for last minute rescue in artwork. Love your work at Meadow Pond Photography.

OTHER BOOKS BY DAVID C. ALVES

A Sabbatical Primer for Pastors: How to Initiate and Navigate a Spiritual Renewal Leave. Createspace, 2013.

We're the 'sons of God' . . . So What?: Believe God About Who You Really Are! New York: iUniverse, June 2009.

Please take a moment to rate and/or comment on this book and add my author page as a favorite for special release updates.

Thank you for Reading

May the Lord Bless and Keep You

CPSIA information can be obtained
at www.ICGtesting.com
Printed in the USA
LVOW02s0021070617

537193LV00009B/152/P